Biblical

Mental

Rehab

Wynndy Wilson

ISBN: 1543185479
ISBN-13: 978-1543185478

DEDICATED TO:

All chaotic, messy minds
who are courageous
enough to become
well-balanced, whole persons.

.

BIBLICAL MENTAL REHAB
TABEL OF CONTENTS:

	Introduction	i
1	The Well-Planned Life	1
2	The Enriched Life	10
3	The Free Life	19
4	The Healing Life	29
5	The Engaged Life	39
6	The Tree of Life	50
7	The Love Life	63
8	The Kingdom Life	71
9	The Listening Life	89
10	The Beautiful Life	97
11	The Surrounded Life	104
12	The Garden Life	122

INTRODUCTION

Most of my life was lived through the threats of fear and anxiety. I was socially awkward and felt like I didn't fit in anywhere. My life was paralyzed by my negative inner voice. I didn't like myself. I wondered how anyone could like me (or love me) if I couldn't find any redeeming value about myself.

No, I didn't grow up in an abusive family. Sure, my family had its shares of depression, anxiety, fear and anger--which shaped my own life. But there's one element that should shock you about my life, but I bet you have the same element as I did.

I grew up going to church three times a week. I attended Vacation Bible School every summer. And I rarely missed a service held during bi-annual revivals. My life was not the replica of 1 Peter 1:8 (ERV): "You have not seen Christ, but still you love him. You can't see him now, but you believe in him. You are filled with a wonderful and heavenly joy that cannot be explained."

I grew up to become a nurse. Although I didn't work in the field, I was intrigued with psychology. I somehow knew that my life didn't add up to what the Bible said about me. I worked as a nurse for 27 years. Toward the end of my nursing career, I told God I wanted to work for him. Well, he allowed circumstances to come about for that wish to come true. I knew I would be writing books and bible studies for him.

But I really wanted to learn how the Bible could change us, mentally. I had heard that the Bible is the best psychology book ever written. So I asked God to show me how the Bible can help us. And I added an extra request--I wanted techniques of how to use the Bible other than just reading it.

I am pleased to tell you that our generously-giving God gave me what I asked for. He gave me plenty of things to help me, things that I will be sharing with you. I have a saying "there's always more with God." And friend, that statement is true, because he has given me information for my second book as well.

So enter this book as if entering an outpatient rehab clinic. It won't cost you an arm and a leg like a rehab clinic would. It will only cost you the price of the book and dedication to read it and be compliant with the recommendations.

Live out Hebrews 11:1 (ERV): "Faith is what makes real the things we hope for. It is proof of what we cannot see." Change is real with the help of God and the Bible! Enjoy!

A WELL-PLANNED LIFE

Chapter One

Last fall I brought all of my houseplants into our tiny apartment. My precious plants wouldn't have stood a chance to survive the snow and freezing temperatures that Boone, NC is famous for. Once I had them inside I carefully arranged them so all could receive the proper lighting needed to thrive. I thought I had positioned all of them in good spots--but one of them didn't survive.

An now it's spring time. Just now, as I'm writing this chapter, I glanced over at the dead sago palm. I had pushed the pot up under a table in order to get it out of the way until I could deal with it in the spring. What I saw gave me a thrill. I noticed a green frond coming out of the pineapple-looking bulb. I immediately poured a glass of water in the pot and pulled it out from under the table so it could receive more light.

Only a fellow plant-lover can understand how I can grieve over a dead plant. Only a fellow plant-lover can understand my delight in the rebirth of a "dead" one. I get more excited over a dead plant coming back to life than I do with my thriving plants. I know, I sound like a crazy person, but it's true. The revival of my tiny sago palm reminds me of the miracle of our own rebirth provided by Jesus.

Do you feel like a thriving, energetic, loving individual? Or do you use adjectives such as "lifeless", "zapped of energy", and "unloved" to describe your life? The daily habits of life can be draining. Life without a clear direction can lead to frustration and dead ends. Why does life have to be this way? I suggest that we take a look back at the beginning to find the answer.

The Giver of Life

The first two chapters of Genesis paint a picture of how God gave us life. He created all of life: plant, animal and human. He created life so that it would produce more life. It was God's plan to give us life with a forward motion of new experiences and new joys. The Garden of Eden was his gift to us--a beautiful, enjoyable place to experience good life.

Genesis 2:7 (NLT) offers more description of his gift of life: "Then the Lord God formed the man from the dust of the ground. He breathed the breath of life into the man's nostrils, and the man became a living person." I wondered why God used dirt from all of the mediums he could have chosen from to form a human being? As I began to think about our messy lives I considered that he had a plan for his choice of mediums.

The Taker of Life

The first two chapters of Genesis deal with life. Chapter three deals with death. Life was good in the Garden of Eden. Adam and Eve had the perfect life--the one you and I fantasize about. The neighborhood was perfect--no crime. Food was abundant--no hunger. The weather forecast was always a good one--no blizzards or hurricanes. Work was an enjoyable experience--not a drudgery. Adam and Eve enjoyed being themselves. They had never experienced bad health or unstable mentality. They enjoyed each other and God. And God even gave them the ability to make choices, which they enjoyed doing--until they made the wrong choice! But why did they make the wrong choice----their life was perfect?

God gave Adam and Eve only one rule to obey. They were instructed not to eat fruit from the Tree of the Knowledge of Good and Evil. It was no big deal. They were not deprived of anything! They just couldn't eat the fruit from that one tree. It was a test from God to see if they would remain loyal to him.

It was quite easy to pass the test. There was no reason not to trust God. And truly they loved him. Then the taker of life entered the Garden. He entered in the form of a snake. Satan approached Eve with the intention of confusing and tricking her. Satan realized if he could get her attention off of God and onto herself that she would be hooked. He convinced Eve that she would not die (which didn't happen immediately) if she ate of the fruit. He convinced her that she would know good and evil, just as the name of the tree implies, if she ate the fruit. Surely knowing good and evil would be a good thing, right? Knowing good (which they already knew) leads to good. But knowing evil (which they hadn't previously known) leads to evil. So when Adam and Eve chose to break God's rule they choose good as well as evil. Evil entered their lives. Evil started the death process.

Don't Worry! We have Good News!

In Mark 16:15-16 (GWT) we find Jesus telling his disciples (as well as you and me) to spread the good news. This is what he said to them: "So wherever you go in the world, tell everyone the Good News. Whoever believes and is baptized will be saved, but whoever does not believe will be condemned." The Message says nonbelievers will be damned. The New Century Version says unbelievers will be punished. People, even Christians, have a hard time accepting the fact that a person could be damned, condemned and punished for not believing in Jesus Christ and who he is. I understand why it is hard to hear those words of death. I, too, don't want anyone to be condemned, damned and punished. And guess what! Neither does God! Just like Adam and Eve, he gives us choices, too. Remember that the knowledge of good leads to good and the knowledge of evil leads to evil. Knowing and believing Jesus leads to good because he is good. Not knowing Jesus leads in the opposite direction, evil. Satan tricks and confuses us just like he did Eve.

Let's revisit Adam and Eve in the Garden. Adam disobeyed God's rule. He and Eve suffered the consequences of their choice--and so did the rest of us. They lost their beautiful home. Work became a drudgery. Hunger was a new thing to experience. But worst of all, they lost intimate contact with God. God could no longer come face to face with them because he cannot look directly on evil. He is a pure and perfect God who created every living thing.

God's love for Adam and Eve didn't change but their feelings toward God did. Everything changed the minute they made the choice to know evil. It would seem that Adam and Eve might know more now than before. But what they didn't anticipate were the effects of evil on every aspect of their lives. Evil brought death into their lives. Death drained the life out of every thought, feeling and action they had. It diminished their ability to think, feel and live a good life. It affects us the same way. One important thing for us to ingrain in our minds is that God is all-knowing. We humans are limited-knowing. So why did God create us knowing that we would make bad choices. Well, God did it with a plan in mind. He had a plan in place to rescue us from the death threat just as soon as we made the wrong choice.

Romans 5:19 (GWT) reveals God's plan: "Clearly, through one person's disobedience humanity became sinful, and through one person's obedience humanity will receive God's approval." Adam disobeyed and Jesus obeyed. Without Jesus, humanity would have remained damned and condemned, experiencing never-ending punishment. Sounds drastic, doesn't it? It is drastic. It would have been tragic and unloving if Father God hadn't provided us with a way to know and experience good and give life back to us.

How is it possible to know good and live a good life? Romans 10:9 (NIRV) tells you how: "Say with your mouth, 'Jesus is Lord.' Believe in your heart that God raised him from the dead. Then you will be saved." This verse clearly says that you need to commit seriously to Jesus in order to have a good life. In fact, you are instructed to speak it, believe it and live it! It is a serious inside to outside commitment to Jesus!

I can sense you have a nagging question. Why did God create us with the ability to choose if he knew we wouldn't choose well? The truth is we were created with the ability to choose--we just didn't choose well. And consider the affect we would have had on God if we didn't have the ability to choose. Programmed love is not true love. There would be no need for test of love or even to proclaim love. Programmed love just doesn't feel the same as chosen love.

Now that the nagging question is out of the way, let's turn our attention to the evil in our lives. There are great benefits to a serious inside to outside commitment to Jesus. Psalm 103:3-5 (NCV) lists the benefits: "He forgives all my sins and heals all my diseases. He saves my life from the grave and loads me with love and mercy. He satisfies me with good things and makes me young again, like the eagle." Wouldn't you like to trade in your messy life for a clean slate? That's exactly what Jesus has done for you! The problem is God's forgiveness is hard for us to accept. We humans don't forgive as easily and freely like Father God does. But that doesn't mean God hasn't forgiven us. The truth is we reject his forgiveness and thus we continue living messy lives. Father knows about our flawed way of thinking. Look at 2 Peter 1:9b (NIRV): "You are blind. You have forgotten that your past sins have been washed away." The truth is our minds have been trained to accept evil as normal. Sometimes we refuse to accept evil as evil. In essence, we are blinded by evil. However, the benefits of our salvation are to heal our blindness and receive the gift of good life!

The key to healing is focusing on Jesus and his teachings. John 15:3 (GNT) refers to this mysterious healing: "You have been made clean already by the teaching I have given you." You don't have to wait to see a counselor or be given a diagnosis by a doctor. Your help has already been provided for you. Lining up your thinking, feeling and actions with his teachings are ways to prove your chosen love for him. You can give up evil and choose his good.

Beware of Bad News

Satan may have permanently lost you to the salvation provided by Jesus but he prefers to have you working for him as long as he can--or as long as you are willing to. John 10:10a (AMP) warns us: "The thief comes only in order to steal and kill and destroy." If you aren't paying attention and careful thought to the direction your life is moving in, chances are you are being killed, destroyed and mugged by Satan. That's why you are experiencing a death-type life. Satan's aim is to keep you helpless and messed up so you won't be telling anyone else about Jesus' Good News. Consider that if your life is a total mess then you don't have the good news to share with anyone. But Jesus intends for you to live the good life as he tells us in the 2nd half of John 10:10 (AMP): "I came that they may have and enjoy life, and have it in abundance (to the full, till it overflows)." This is completely the opposite of what Satan wants you to believe. Remember how he confused and tricked Eve? He's doing the same thing to you, too!

Exchange the American Dream for God's Dream

Are you living the American dream? Most of us think the American dream is to own our own home. Owning a home is a good dream and it's my dream. Owning a home would make me very happy. But the American dream is more than owning a home. If you were to research the original thought behind the American dream you would discover that it's a social idea. Anyone who believes in the American dream feels there should be equality of life across the board: politically, financially and socially. Did you notice that Jesus is left out of this dream? Satan managed to trick a whole nation with his lies.

The American dream doesn't work in God's reality. He created us to be different from each other. Our fingerprints and DNA are proof of this. The same goes for our personality traits. Family histories, life experiences and religious upbringings shape who we are. For that reason, all Americans (or any other nationality) cannot be placed in the same political, social or financial dream. Add on the different gifts and talents to the personalities. God produces a wide variety of people, families, communities and nations. Variety is not a bad thing. It is a God thing. But somehow, the American dream has declared, "being different" as "being bad." All I can do is shake my head at Satan. Wouldn't it be a boring America if we all had the same ideas and aspirations? It would be like living in a nation with only one American sized subdivision--all the houses looking alike. It would be difficult to give directions to your home--there would be no distinguishing landmarks.

Having a dream is not a bad thing if you know what to dream. A dream is a strongly desired goal or purpose. God has a goal and purpose just for you. That includes a life filled to the brim and overflowing with goodness and abundance, just like Adam and Eve experienced in Eden. The American dream limit's a person's goals. Think about it.

So what is God's dream for us? A well-loved bible verse describes it. Jeremiah 29:11 (NIV) says: "For I know the plans I have for you, declares the Lord, plans to prosper you and not to harm you, plans to give you a hope and a future." Those folks who have death-type lives are drawn to this verse. A death-type person doesn't have any goals or purposes and this verse promises a plan.

Consider the effect of a lone word in this verse. The word "plan" changes your mental path. Imagine how a whole book full of hope-type words could change your life. Now I want to bring you to a new reality. It's God's reality. Notice the plans belong to God and are handed out by God. Please don't shut down. I know you like being in control of your life, but acknowledge that you haven't done such a good job. And there are some people who will not relate to the "prosper" part of this verse. Prosperity feels like a dirty sin to some people. That's a good trick played on you by Satan. He's good at what he does. But God wants his money to be in his children's hands. He trusts his children to help the needy.

Remember Where You Came From

It is my belief that God chose to create us from dirt for two reasons. The first reason is that dirt is the lowliest form of all mediums. He wants us to compare our present messy lives to the medium he created us from. Just as he first created good human beings from dirt, he is able to rise up a new, good life out of your messiness.

The second reason is that dirt is a growing medium. Grass, vegetables, flowers and trees grow out of dirt. Dirt delivers nutrients and moisture to the plant life. Consider the varying heights of plant life that emerges out of the dirt. Our lives are a garden of sorts for the gifts, talents, teachings and plans Father has for us. What plant life can you compare your life to? Are you soft yet spreading like a lawn full of grass? Are your vines producing fruit? And are you standing tall and strong like a tree? Chapter 12 of this book is a special chapter. It's called The Garden Life. Read on through the whole book and put into practice the things you will learn. By the time you reach The Garden Life you'll know the dreams God has for you.

What is Life?

Webster's dictionary explains life as the period from birth to death. It also says that physical and mental experiences make up the existence of an individual. Would you be surprised to find out that Webster includes that life is the spiritual existence that transcends physical death? So the human life is made up of three dimensions: physical, mental and spiritual. We tend to limit our thoughts of life to that of the physical area. But I believe we view life totally backwards. John 6:63 (GWT) refers to the foundation of our lives: "Life is spiritual. Your physical existence doesn't contribute to that life. The words that I have spoken to you are spiritual. They are life." Now consider how the mental life regulates the physical life as found in Proverbs 16:24 (AMP): "Pleasant words are as a honeycomb, sweet to the mind and healing to the body."

How do you feel about Jesus' claim that his words are life? If you choose to give it a chance, God's word can change your life by changing your believing, thinking, feelings and your actions. All of these elements control your physical life. I have experienced healing from his word and will share it with you later. Your life may be messy because you have suffered tragedy, molestation, abandonment, lies, etc. The wonderful book called the Bible declares that these events are in your past, not your future. Father knows you are broken from the evil things done to you but he didn't leave you alone to deal with it. He sent Jesus, the giver of new life, to rescue you from the old messy one.

What is Death?

Webster says to be dead means to be deprived of life, lacking power or effect, no longer having interest, relevance or significance. Sounds a lot like depression to me. I usually equate death and deadness with cessation of a beating heart. I guess there really is such a thing as the walking dead. That's what sin does to the human life. It drains the life out of every aspect of it.

Adam and Eve didn't die immediately, physically that is. But they suffered deadness as described by Webster. You, too, may suffer from mental and spiritual deadness but you don't have to remain dead. Jesus Christ has given you a choice that can undo the choice Adam and Eve made for you. Deuteronomy 30:19 (GWT) declares it: "I call on heaven and earth as witnesses today that I have offered you life or death, blessings or curses. Choose life so that you and your descendants will live." And verse 20 tells how you can choose life: "Love the Lord your God, obey him and be loyal to him. This will be your way of life, and it will mean a long life for you."

The Father of Your Life

Most people don't recognize God as a good and loving father. They think he is mean and makes life hard. Do you feel as though he is angry with you? Do you have to earn his love? Allow Psalm 103:8, 10-12 (NLT) to challenge your view of him: "The Lord is compassionate and merciful, slow to get angry and filled with unfailing love. He does not punish us for all our sins; he does not deal harshly with us, as we deserve. For his unfailing love toward those who fear him is as great as the height of the heavens above the earth." Guess who God deals harshly with? He hates evil and the evil spirits that spreads evil--Satan who has made your life miserable. That's who his wrath is intended for.

God is the best father you could ever want. He'll lead you right and not disappoint you. Don't you enjoy following a leader who seems bigger than life, has more answers than you have questions, is stable, confident, and firm and motivates people? The very things you enjoy and look for in a leader are the characteristics of your Father, the Lord our God!

Jesus has a few more words of advice to give you. Matthew 11:28-30 (MSG): "Are you tired? Worn out? Burned out on religion? Come to me. Get away with me and you'll recover your life. I'll show you how to take a real rest. Walk with me and work with me--watch how I do it. Learn the unforced rhythms of grace. I won't lay anything heavy or ill fitting on you. Keep company with me and you'll learn to live freely and lightly."

THE ENRICHED LIFE

Chapter Two

I describe most of my life as painfully shy and socially awkward. I didn't like who I was (or wasn't). I felt invisible, unimportant and voiceless. It was as if I were a nonperson. This nonperson was unable to do many normal things.

Looking back, I can see how Satan tricked me into thinking that I was diminished and disabled. He didn't want me to grow into the person I am today. He didn't want me to share Jesus' good news. But I am and so can you!

A Peek into My Future

Join me in a trip back in time. Welcome to my teenage years! Momma and Daddy faithfully took us kids to church every Sunday morning, Sunday night and Wednesday night. Don't be surprised to find out that I come from a family of God communicators. My Daddy became a pastor in my teenage years and Momma typed up his sermons. My youngest brother, Drew, is the current pastor of my childhood church. We can learn a lot about who we are and what we are gifted to do by looking at our family.

I want to introduce you to my childhood pastor. We called him Preacher Alton. I describe Preacher Alton Williams as being very traditional. He didn't do much out of the ordinary. However, one year he did something unusual. Always pay attention to unusual features--God gets our attention by using these events. Preacher Alton met with several of us teenagers and handed out topics for us to speak on. That meant standing up on the pulpit in front of 150 people and speak on an assigned topic. I am still amazed that I was not freaked out by this assignment due to my extreme shyness. Again, pay attention to the unusual. Truthfully, I was a little nervous, but not overwhelmingly so.

After church, I took the piece of paper home and thought about the two words written on it. I should have been panicking about the topic because I didn't know much about it. I had knowledge about it but couldn't explain it. Mysteriously, I wasn't scared.

We didn't have the internet or multiple bible translations back in the 70's. That means I pulled out the KJV bible and turned to the concordance in the back of it. If you don't get anything out of this book, please remember this--to use the concordance in the back of your bible. It will steer you in the direction you need to go in. It helped me out. I found several passages relating to the Holy Spirit. I read all of the verses I could find.

We were given assigned days to speak and my big day arrived. Preacher Alton looked over at the choir section where I was sitting and called me up. I remember feeling a few butterflies in my stomach but that didn't affect my march up to the podium. I felt strangely calm as I looked down at the 150 pairs of eyes looking back at me. My report was relatively short but I delivered it with confidence. I relayed to my listeners that Holy Spirit is the Spirit of God who lives inside of us. He moves in the moment we receive Jesus' salvation. I continued to tell them that we can't see Him but we can feel Him. He directs us, comforts us and counsels us. I felt good about the presentation and others confirmed my feelings. I received compliments and surprising reactions at how composed and calm I was.

That event was a peek into my future as a God communicator. One of the jobs of Holy Spirit is to give us spiritual gifts--which I did not mention that day. He presented my gift in an unusual and audible way, using my voice. Do you remember the statement I made about feeling voiceless?

Back to My Normal
Oddly enough, that boost from Holy Spirit didn't change my

life. I still felt invisible, voiceless and unimportant. A nagging question pops up: since Holy Spirit was living inside of me, why didn't he continue to empower me, especially after the boost? The fact that he gave me a boost is proof that he was willing to work through me and use me. Evidently, the problem had to be with me.

So, why did Father God use a nonperson at that particular time? Funny enough, as a nonperson, I didn't even consider backing out and refusing to participate in the assignment. I believe a good reason is that Holy Spirit used a known socially shy girl to speak boldly and confidently. One could say that "I was not acting like myself" and one would be right and wrong. My true self (the one enriched by Holy Spirit) used the gift of speaking that was already within me. My false self (shy, invisible and voiceless) melted away as I allowed Holy Spirit to enrich me--even though it was just for 15 minutes while I gave the speech.

Holy Spirit knows us intimately and personally. He knows things about us that we aren't aware of ourselves. In fact, I didn't recognize my gift of communication until a few years ago, during my middle-aged years.

Allow me to introduce Holy Spirit to you and share a few more facts this time around, than I did back in the 70's.

*Holy Spirit moves into our lives the moment we commit to Jesus Christ. Two verses verify this fact. Ephesians 1:13b (NIRV): "When you believed, he marked you with a seal. The seal is the Holy Spirit that he promised." And 2 Corinthians 6:19 (NCV): "You should know that your body is a temple for the Holy Spirit who is in you. You have received the Holy Spirit from God so you do not belong to yourselves." Two things happened at the moment of your salvation. Jesus rescued you from death. He also requested Father to give Holy Spirit to you to live inside of you and help you live a good life. Holy Spirit is our connection to God. When you pray to God, he gives Holy Spirit commands in order to respond to your requests.

*Holy Spirit gives you a new identification. Ephesians 4:30 (NLT): "And do not bring sorrow to God's Holy Spirit by the way you live. Remember, he is the one who has identified you as His own, guaranteeing that you will be saved on the day of redemption." The truth is Holy Spirit was not happy with my nonperson self. The other truth is, I didn't grasp the reality of the real me. I didn't take the opportunity to exchange my old life for the new one.

*Holy Spirit has deep feelings for you and is ready to help you even when you don't know how to help yourself. Romans 8:26 (NCV): "Also, the Spirit helps us with our weakness. We do not know how to pray as we should. But the Spirit Himself speaks to God for us, even begs God for us with deep feelings that words cannot explain." Holy Spirit loves us despite the messy lives we live in. No problem is too big or too messy for him.

*Holy Spirit approaches us while still in a state of needing to be rescued. John 16:8 (AMP): "And when He comes, He will convict and convince the world and bring demonstration to it about sin and about righteousness (uprightness of heart and right standing with God) and about judgment." Holy Spirit is well acquainted with Satan. He knows all of his tricks and lies. Holy Spirit loves you too much not to warn you of Satan's antics. At the same time, he knows who you really are, minus the false parts that Satan has lied to you about. Holy Spirit communicates with you and uses God's words to point things out that need to be corrected.

*He teaches us and increases our intelligence. John 14:26 (NIRV): "But the Father will send the Friend in my name to help you. The Friend is the Holy Spirit. He will teach you all things. He will remind you of everything I have said to you." Consider this thought: your best friend is living inside of you. You two are never separated. He loves you and is teaching you how to live a good life.

*Holy Spirit channels love, power, and personal control into our lives. 2 Timothy 1:7 (AMP): "For God did not give us a spirit of timidity (of cowardice, of craven and cringing and fawning fear), but [he has given us a spirit] of power and of love and of calm and well-balanced mind and discipline and self-control." I've read this verse hundreds of times but I didn't take it seriously. I 'duly-noted" it and mentally filed it away. But I experienced all of these gifts the day I gave my speech--so it is to be taken seriously!

*Holy Spirit speaks to our minds. Romans 9:1 (NIRV): "I speak the truth in Christ. I am not lying. My mind tells me that what I say is true. It is guided by the Holy Spirit." The more you open up your mind to the Holy Spirit the more you'll hear him. Treat him as the personal companion that he is.

*Holy Spirit gives us extra gifts to live God's way--and it's an excellent way to live! Galatians 5:22-23 (MSG): "But what happens when we live God's way? He brings gifts into our lives, much the same way that fruit appears in an orchard--things like affection for others, exuberance about life, serenity. We develop a willingness to stick with things, a sense of compassion in the heart, and a conviction that a basic holiness permeates things and people. We find ourselves involved in loyal commitments, not needing to force our way in life, able to marshal and direct our energies wisely." Don't you crave this kind of life? It beats the messy one to pieces!

*Holy Spirit gives us gifts that reflect our personality types and ministries. Romans 12:6-8 (NLT): "God has given each of us the ability to do certain things well. So if God has given you the ability to prophesy, speak out when you have faith that God is speaking through you. If your gift is that of serving others, serve them well. If you are a teacher, do a good job of teaching. If your gift is to encourage others, do it! If you have money, share it generously. If God has given you leadership ability, take the responsibility seriously. And if you have a gift for showing kindness to others, do it gladly." Did you spot your gift from this list? My gift is of communication, speaking, writing and teaching as evidenced by the experience in my teenage years. I also have secondary gifts of encouragement and kindness. I have had occasions to serve, give and lead. I performed these gifts to the best of my ability with Holy Spirit's help. Several bible verses explain that the more you give or do, the better you perform. Forget average. You are now enriched to super perform. Do away with procrastination. Just do it!

Three Part You

Our creator uses examples all over the bible. One example is the similarity of you compared to God. Genesis chapter one reports that we are created in Their image. We were created by three beings: Father God, Jesus the Son, and the Friend, the Holy Spirit. So it should come as no surprise that you are made up of three living parts. Body, soul and spirit.

The body is our physical life--the one that sees, hears, touches, smells, tastes and speaks. It also behaves. 1 Corinthians 15:40 (GNT) holds an interesting observation about our bodies: "And there are heavenly bodies and earthly bodies, the beauty that belongs to heavenly bodies is different from the beauty that belongs to earthly bodies."

The soul is our mental life--the one that thinks, wills (reject or refuse), and feels (emotions). The soul and spirit are often used interchangeably but they are different in function.

The spirit is our communication life between us and our creators. It is the part of us that experiences relationship with God, Jesus and Holy Spirit. It is the site that receives power, love and energy from Holy Spirit. Hebrews 4:12 tells us that the soul and spirit are in close proximity of each other. It is my thought that they are perhaps attached to or beside each other. Our spirit is the center of our belief system and is obedient to whichever spirit it chooses to listen to and believe in. That means you are either obedient to Holy Spirit or evil spirit. Your belief system feeds into your thinking system (soul). The thinking system produces emotion. And emotions project out in behavior and actions. Behaviors and actions affect our physical health.

The True Essence of Our Lives

Jesus taught his disciples in a personal, face to face manner. I am envious of those disciples but I shouldn't be. Jesus has gifted us with a closer personal, face-to-face experience than what the disciples had. Listen to John 14:26 (MSG): "The Friend, the Holy Spirit, whom the Father will send at my request, will make everything plain to you. He will remind you of all the things I have told you. I'm leaving you well and whole." Jesus gifted us with his presence 24/7, 365. He has given us supernatural closeness and access. Why did he gift us with such extravagance? According to John 14:26 it is to help us to live in health, wellbeing and wholeness! I like to say that God is the giver of life, Jesus is the giver of new life and Holy Spirit is the giver of healthy life.

Are you tapping into the amazing life that Holy Spirit wants to help you live? I love the motivation of Romans 15:13 (MSG): "Oh! May the God of green hope fill you up with joy; fill you up with peace, so that your believing lives, filled with the life-giving energy of the Holy Spirit, will brim over with hope." Those of you who are tired and lifeless may be wondering how to tap into the life-giving energy of the Holy Spirit. The clue is in the middle of the verse: "your believing lives." It requires you to give consent to yourself to believe in Holy Spirit and listen to him as he speaks to your spirit. Rejecting the advice of Holy Spirit means that you are accepting advise from evil spirit. In essence, you have yourself to blame for your messy life.

The Gift of Faith

Confidence is the foundation of a healthy belief system. How do you determine what you have confidence in? You may claim that your feelings determine your confidence. If this is your claim, I advise you to travel backwards. This strange piece of advice will expose what your core beliefs are based on. State what your feelings are toward any given thing. Next, ask yourself what thought energizes these feelings? Then, what belief made you have this thought? Let me give you an example: I love watching Fox News. So, why do I love watching Fox News? My thought centers on their claim to report the truth. I have confidence in and believe them when they claim to report the truth. Therefore, my beliefs fuel my thoughts and my thoughts direct my emotions and my emotions propel my action to watch their news.

Faith and belief are gifts from God. We are not designed to initiate faith. I asked you in the last paragraph what you have confidence in. Take note that something has to exist outside of yourself to direct confidence to. Self-confidence doesn't work (even though we try to make it so) because there has to be a standard to compare to. If we chose to find confidence in ourselves then no one else really matters because their standard would have to measure up to ours and not the other way around. Perhaps this explanation will help you understand the meaning of Ephesians 2:8 (NLT): "God saved you by his grace when you believed. And you can't take credit for this; it is a gift from God."

More Gifts of Faith

We receive the gift of faith at the moment of our salvation. The foundation of our confidence begins at this moment with room to grow. Our lives are not frozen in one moment of time (time of salvation). Sadly, lots of folks choose to remain mentally frozen in that one moment of time. Their faith is stunted and stifled. The bible refers to these folks as babies in Christ. They are not growing spiritually.

If the above statement describes you, there are steps you can take to stimulate your spiritual growth and health. Romans 10:7

(MSG) says to listen to Holy Spirit: "The point is, before you trust, you have to listen. But unless Christ's word is preached, there's nothing to listen to."

According to Mark 9:24b (NCV) the next step is to ask for help: "I do believe! Help me to believe more!"

Consider that there are different levels of faith as stated in 1 Corinthians 12:9a (GWT): "To another person the same Spirit gives courageous faith." Other translations call it great faith and wonder-working faith. I like to refer to the different levels of faith as: 1. Casual faith. This is the faith when you know who God is but have a casual approach to him. 2. Confident faith. This faith is a strong faith. It shows you are close to God and love him. 3. Courageous faith. You are very intimate with God and would do anything for him

The last paragraph might suggest that Father plays favorites with his children. But that's just not true. He wants all of us to have courageous, wonder-working faith. Those who receive the wonder-working faith are those who seriously want it.

Confident Belief

It is Satan's desire that you think he is bigger and more powerful than God. And you believe him or you wouldn't be living a messy life. It is true that Satan can cause havoc in your life, but he's not God. Listen to God's claim in Jeremiah 32:27 (NIV): "I am the Lord, the God of all mankind. Is anything too hard for me?" The answer is a big NO! And that includes making good out of Satan's bad. Whatever messiness you are now living in, God can make wonderfulness out of it, believe it or not.

The Best Life

And now a word of advice from Father in Romans 12:1-2 (MSG): "So here's what I want you to do, God helping you: Take your everyday, ordinary life--your sleeping, eating, going-to-work, and walking-around life--and place it before God as an offering. Embracing what God does for you is the best thing you can do for Him. Don't become so well adjusted to your culture that you fit into it without even thinking. Instead, fix your attention on God. You'll be changed from the inside out. Readily recognize what he wants from you, and quickly respond to it. Unlike the culture around you, always dragging you down to its level of immaturity,

God brings the best out of you, develops well-formed maturity in you."

THE FREE LIFE

Chapter Three

Memorial Day is a day marked on the calendar for the purpose of celebrating the brave men and women who died fighting for our American freedom. Memorial Day is a time when American families, friends and neighbors gather. Some gather at a memorial wall. Others visit gravesites. Almost all unite at a designated home for a cookout and relationship time. Gratitude and American pride is felt from coast to coast.

American freedom has afforded us to be able to worship any religion we choose. It allows us to speak openly. We Americans have rights that not many other countries share. We are so blessed and gifted with good things from God!

We know what American freedom is, but do you know what spiritual freedom is? It may be easier to explain what the opposite of it is--spiritual obstruction. A follower of Jesus Christ who is not living the free life is obstructed by wrong beliefs. A spiritual obstructed life is characterized by frenzied thinking, out-of-control emotions, stubbornness and self-centeredness. This person is overwhelmed by negativity and is unable to feel hope or satisfaction. If you are living a spiritually obstructed life, I encourage you to hang on because we are going to discover a way to remove the obstruction. How can I declare this so confidently? Because God said it is so in Romans 8:23 (NCV): "We also have been waiting with pain inside us. We have the Spirit as the first part of God's promise. So we are waiting for God to finish making us his own children, which means our bodies will be made free."

Why are You Obstructed?

Everybody deals with messiness at one time or another, or perhaps all the time. I've encountered messy people at work, church, school, on TV, and even in my own home--a finger pointing at me. The messiness follows us wherever we go. That's because the messiness starts in our minds, souls and spirits. The Good News is that God wants to finish making us his children so we can be free in our minds, souls and spirits. The waiting can be over if you choose it to be. The choosing starts in your mind.

Believe it or not (and please do believe this statement), you have chosen to be obstructed. Yes, that's right! You have permitted the bad things that are blocking God's good things in your life. Jesus tells us what those things are in John 8:34b (MSG): "I tell you most solemnly that anyone who chooses a life of sin is trapped in a dead-end life and is, in fact, a slave." Adam and Eve made a choice that resulted in behaviors against God. Those behaviors, known as sin, have been passed down to us. I don't know about you, but I have made sin an important factor in my life. Let me explain before you get the wrong idea. There are times I have sinned and times I have prevented myself from sinning. I'm guilty of working very diligently not to sin. That means I focused more on not sinning than I did on Jesus. Jesus dealt with my sin and cleaned me up but I kept it alive through shame and guilt and a constant mindset not to sin. Sin became my god.

Did you realize that there is a moment when sin is not a sin? Don't get upset with me just yet. Let me explain and listen to James 1:15 (AMP): "Then the evil desire, when it has conceived, gives birth to sin, and sin, when it is fully matured, brings forth death." The conception, birth and maturity of sin take place in the mind and proceeds to the physical life as behavior. An evil desire can enter your mind without being conceived. A bad thought can pop in your thinking system and you can refuse to implant it in your mind. Dwelling and mulling over bad things produces a bad life.

What is it about us that allow such a bad thing to be implanted in our minds? Back up to James 1:14 (AMP): "But every person is tempted when he is drawn away, enticed and baited by his own evil desire (lust, passions)." Self usually gets what self-wants, don't you agree? Self usually doesn't know what's best for self but that's an argument you'll lose to self. Please consider the truthfulness to the last statement.

Pride is a tricky subject. The church culture I grew up in taught us not to have, feel or display any kind of pride. This was their way of teaching us how to be humble. I'll talk about my idea of how to be humble later, but let's look at the issue of pride. Pride can be a good thing as well as a bad thing. Satan was the first one to use pride in the wrong way. It was in fact his first evil act. Pride got him thrown out of heaven and out of God's presence. Allow God to show you how he wants you to feel pride in a good, healthy way. Listen to God in Matthew 3:17 (TLB): "And a voice from heaven said, 'This is my beloved Son, and I am wonderfully pleased with him.'" God felt immense pride in his Son and he feels the same about us.

One of my new favorite verses (I find new ones all the time) is Galatians 6:4 (GWT): "Each of you must examine your own actions. Then you can be proud of your own accomplishments without comparing yourself to others." Our confusion (because we have listened to Satan) about pride keeps us from doing what this verse says to do. We become frustrated with our lives. We turn on others and criticize their actions instead of evaluating ourselves. That leads us to compare ourselves to everyone else. The life that God intended for us to live gets lost in the circle of confusion. Please know that it's ok to be proud of the life God has given you. Now read on to verse 5 (NCV): "Each person must be responsible for himself." Living a good God life is your responsibility! In fact, he tells us in Hebrews 4:13b (NIRV): "He will hold us responsible for everything we do." Or don't do. Living a good God life is a command. You have permission, better yet, a command, to enjoy your life and grow it to its God fullness. I see that smile on your face. Don't you love Good News?

Now we have to clear up the humble thing. My husband, Keevin, and I moved away from our families after we were married. We both found ourselves in a new church culture. I didn't learn the truth about how to be humble right away but I discovered new ways to look at what the Bible said. I learned not to take what others said as biblical. The problem we have is some of our beliefs have been passed down for so many generations that those past-down beliefs sound biblical. That's because the beliefs are laced with biblical truth. Do you recognize that this is a trick of the Devil? He copies the behavior of Jesus Christ and disguises his lies with small elements of truth--the bible says so.

To be humble means to submit, surrender to God. We have a hard time doing this because we want to keep control of our own lives. I also think it's hard to do because it feels like we'd just disappear if we go any lower than we already are. But what's in it for us? Alot, my friend! James 4:10 (NLT) explains: "Humble yourselves before the Lord, and he will lift you up in honor." That statement means that God doesn't leave us in a lowly place.

Unworthiness is one way Satan gets sin in your mind. God designed us to feel worth. Adam and Eve didn't know what unworthiness was--until they chose to listen to Satan. Another way sin enters your mind is to feel doubt. Satan wants you to doubt that God loves you, accepts you and gives you worth. Satan knows he can kill and destroy you and steal your worth if you doubt God's love. Just remember, Satan is not your friend. He is your enemy and is bluffing you!

Satan dangles temptations of self-worth in front of us. We, like Eve, are easily enticed and take the bait. Our society, as well as the church culture, have bought into the idea that our worth comes from within ourselves. Self-worth and self-love are the total opposite of being humble and submissive. It buys into Satan's favorite sin of pride.

Another sin formed in the mind is that of escapisms. He uses it as bait to redirect us from our pain of unworthiness. The escape gives us relief for a while. Porn, fantasies, emotional and physical affairs are a few of the escapes.

A very strong mind-type sin that the Devil uses is paranoia. It works well as a means to drive us further into despair and away from God. Paranoia seems to take away all hope and control. But remember, Holy Spirit lives in you and he is your source of power and hope. You have the power to resist Satan's manipulations.

Satan uses pain to push us farther into darkness. Note that Satan doesn't offer to take our pain away. Escapisms, paranoia and self-help are short-lived and don't offer real resolve. These sins make the pain incredibly worse. However, God wants to take the pain away! Imagine being pain-free! Psalm 116:16 (NIRV) tells us this wonderful news: "Lord, I serve you. I serve you just as my mother did. You have set me free from the chains of my suffering." The mean old Devil keeps us chained up by the pain. Pain can be physical, mental and spiritual. Could it be that you'd rather escape pain (mentally and physically) than have it removed?

Did you know that sin is the cause of pain? Look at Genesis 3:16b, 17b (NIV): "to the woman he said, 'I will make your pains in child bearing very severe; with painful labor you will give birth to children!' 'Cursed is the ground because of you; through painful toil you will eat food from it all the days of your life!'" Pay attention the next time you have a fearful thought. Notice the ping of pain in your heart area. That ping of pain is a signal from God that fear is not a good thing for you to participate in. Bad thinking and bad believing leads to bad pain.

Pills mask pain. Pain masks sin. Sin masks the real you. Who would you be without fear? Who would you be without anger? Who would you be without sinful pride? It seems right to be feeling these emotions at the time, but consider that they don't accomplish satisfaction and long-term health.

Take a mental look at what others see when they look at a person masked in sin. Those who suffer from sinful pride appear as superior and unable to show compassion to others. An angry person develops a blood-red face when spewing rage. Shaky hands, shifting eyes and indecisiveness describes a fearful person. There are two characteristics that are blaringly absent: courage and confidence. These masked people appear cowardly and wimpy. But Father wants you to know that cowardly and wimpy do not describe the real you! Father encourages you in Deuteronomy 31:6 (AMP): "Be strong, courageous and firm; fear not nor be in terror before them." Father doesn't expect you to be strong from your powers. He wants you to be strong from his powers.

Crazy Fear

Fear can cause us to freeze up or it can send us into a spiraling frenzy known as anxiety. Have you ever become paralyzed by fear when in a confrontation? The Good News is that it is possible to engage in a confrontation without becoming mentally paralyzed. Freedom is achieved by dealing with the root of fear. It may surprise you to find out there is such a thing as pseudo anxiety. I hate it when I suffer a panic attack just to find out I imagined a danger that didn't exist. Can you relate? The false danger only existed in my thoughts--it started in my mind. I fell for Satan's temptation (instead of refusing it) just like Eve did. And friend, worrying is not a badge of honor or a personality trait. It's a stealer, killer and destroyer of life.

You may be wondering how to deal with the frozen fear, spiraling anxiety and death-trap worry. The answer is found in Philippians 4:12 (AMP): "...I have learned in any and all circumstances the secret of facing every situation..." The apostle Paul wants to share his secret with you in verse 13 (NCV): "I can do all things through Christ, because he gives me strength." You've heard this verse so many times that you may have not grasped the secret. In fact, the secret is in both verses 12 and 13. I bet you zoomed in on the part where Christ gives us strength--and that is a good part--but what does he give us strength to do? Fear's job is to keep you from facing the bad situations and bad conditions. Your unwillingness to allow Jesus to help you face the bad things in your life cause you to remain frozen, spiraling out of control and in a death trap. What Satan doesn't want you to know is that facing a situation helps to resolve it, to end the pain.

Resolve may mean thanking God for it and trusting him to take care of it without you doing anything. Why Thank God for it? Because we are instructed to do so. Philippians 4:6 (NIRV) tells us to give thanks: "Don't worry about anything. No matter what happens, tell God about everything. Ask and pray, and give thanks to him." It may sound like strange advise but God knows how he wired us mentally. An amazing thing happens when we thank God for the bad things. Being thankful for a bad thing forces us to face it with a sense of confidence. Thankfulness leads us on a positive mental path. Perhaps you won't notice, but thankfulness steers us toward trust in God and his plans for the situation. And from there, we turn onto a path of empathy for others. If you don't believe me, give it a try with your current bad sitution--because I know you have one. Now look at verse 7: "Then God's peace will watch over your hearts and your minds. He will do this because you belong to Christ Jesus. God's peace can never be completely understood." Right there he explains that thankfulness affects your mental health. We discount so many instructions in the bible because we don't have a good mind-grasp of them. I hope everyone will be convinced to do what God's word says even though it can't be explained, at least for now.

"Do not fear" is one of those instructions we tend to discount. It seems to be easier to give in to it than to fight it. Who could have given us the idea that we have to fight fear? Timothy gives us the answer in 2 Timothy 1:7 (AMP): "For God did not give us a spirit of timidity (of cowardice, of craven and cringing and fawning fear), but [He has given us a Spirit] of power and love and of calm and well-balanced mind and discipline and self-control." Note that self-control is a gift of the Spirit and not from self. Would you be surprised to find out that the first negative emotion Adam and Eve felt was fear? God didn't design us to feel fear. Fear is implanted in the mind and acts as a bully. It won't let love in. It won't let you think intelligibly. It makes you unsettled and unstable. It makes your life a mess! Father is telling you here to exchange your fear for his love, power and well-balanced mind. You don't have to fight it, just exchange it. Shift the focus of your mind to him.

Another crazy thing about fear is we equate fear with being unloved. Our fears of rejection, abandonment, failure, etc. come from a root of not feeling loved. God never removes his love from us even though some humans may refuse to give us love. Listening to unloving humans cost us a free life--that's what Romans 6:20 (MSG) says: "As long as you did what you felt like doing, ignoring God, you didn't have to bother with right thinking or right living, or right anything for that matter. But do you call that a free life?"

But what if you are afraid of God? I understand why you might feel this way. After all, the bible calls him a judge who executes wrath. Consider this crazy fact about fear of God--a judge doesn't just rule in negative cases. A judge declares a situation as good or bad. Justice is the act of assigning truthfulness. It steers us toward a positive outcome. A judge ultimately wants good for everyone. A judge can offer a reward for good behavior as well as assigning discipline for bad behavior. God allows consequences in order to steer us in his direction, to his love. His main desire is for us to accept his love and to love him back. He doesn't want you to be afraid of him. God wants you to love him. The bible translates the fear of God as reverence and respect--like the kind you would direct to your loving daddy. Father God wants your love for him to be your focus instead of fear.

Crazy Love

Fear, and anything else that takes our focus off God, is sin or behavior against God. Sin causes us to turn our backs on God. The judgment for bad behavior against God is death. But Father God wants us to have life. He wants us to turn around, face Him and choose to listen to Him. 1 John 1:9 (NIRV) explains how to face him: "But God is faithful and fair. If we admit that we have sinned, he will forgive us our sins. He will forgive every wrong thing we have done. He will make us pure." That verse says His judgment becomes good life to all who choose him.

Crazy Rebellion

We humans are rebellious. We resist advise from God, other humans, and sometimes our own bad experiences. Webster says rebellion is usually unsuccessful. It doesn't make sense why we are rebellious. Good advice is meant to improve our lives. I believe our rebellion is rooted from pride and selfishness. Fear causes a person to guard themselves from possible (not probable) danger. Thus, self-preservation is born, a sin is born. The notion of self-preservation is a big lie--you can't save yourself. You are going to die, it's a fact! So give up the self-preservation theory. Some folks have been hurt by humans and don't trust anyone. They only have confidence in themselves. Weigh this thought out: how can you have confidence in yourself when you didn't create yourself? The truth is you don't have anything to do with your existence or demise. You are here because of another being (God) chose to put you here. You are here because of him and for his purposes.

Some people claim to dislike change. You may think change is bad. You're going to think I'm crazy, but I love change. I get bored easily and welcome a change of scenery, pace, or situation. But for you non-change people, I ask you to be willing to look at all your options (or rather God's option). Look at the experience as if you were shopping for a house. People choose homes that make them happy and where they can experience family love. They choose the one that would benefit them the most. How could you not choose God's option? He offers better (the best) benefits than what you are currently living in.

I imagine there are some of you who blame others for your messy life. You think you have control over the one whom you blame by withholding forgiveness. You just don't want to give up that control. But friend, how do you expect to get your messy life in order while you have a concentrated focus on someone else's life? In effect, you are ignoring and abusing your own life. You are making yourself into a nonperson.

Could it be that you are afraid to live a life of health and freedom? It seems to me that you are refusing to give up your identity of life with pain and chains.

Good Benefits

God created us to be results oriented. That's why good behavior is rewarded with good life and bad behavior is disciplined with bad life. Bad life is meant to direct us to good behavior and good life. God really does want you to have a good life.

Beliefs in general produce results. Bad beliefs, such as degrading statements made about you, result in bad life. Good beliefs, such as God's good word, result in good life.

A belief is the acceptance by the mind that something is true. Romans 10:10 (AMP) explains the concept of belief and its effect: "For with the heart a person believes (adheres to, trusts in, and relies on Christ) and so is justified (declared righteous, acceptable to God), and with the mouth he confesses (declares openly and speaks out freely his faith) and confirms [his] salvation." Your belief in Jesus automatically gets you declared right and acceptable to God. He's the only one who matters!

Salvation begins with a belief as spoken of in Romans 10:9 (NCV): "If you use your mouth to say 'Jesus is Lord,' and if you believe in your heart that God raised him from the dead, you will be saved." Salvation is the beginning of a life saved from bad behaviors against God, from sin. That means you are rescued, rehabbed, recovered, transformed and healed. Salvation is not only the beginning of the new, free life. It lasts a lifetime. However, many folks don't receive the full benefits of their rescue, rehab, recovery, transformation and healing.

Just so that you know, Satan didn't like it when you were saved, but since you are, the next best thing he can do is convince you to stay in pain and chains. Satan knows that your new, free life will inspire others to seek out the same kind of life with God. He hates God. Peter gives stern advise to you in 1 Peter 1:18-19 (MSG): "It cost God plenty to get you out of that dead-end, empty-headed life you grew up in. He paid with Christ's sacred blood, you know. He died like an unblemished, sacrificial lamb." Dear reader, you now have free life care, courtesy of Jesus. Please use it! Claim it! Celebrate it! Live it! Grow it!

Your New Free Spiritual Life

God advises us all throughout the bible to memorize verses. This method is the easiest way to implant God's life-changing thoughts and advise. I started memorizing verses a few years ago, that applied to some troubled areas of my life. I made sure the first verse was Luke 10:27, to love him with my total being. I experienced a strange phenomenon after taking up this practice. I started thinking God-thoughts, automatically, without trying. It occurred all day long during my everyday routine tasks. I was quite delighted with the benefit and felt closer to God.

I have compiled a list of 20 core verses that I have memorized. I often recite these as I lay down at night. I can barely get to number 10 before I fall asleep. Did you anticipate that benefit?

During times of a stressful situation, I will mentally go through my list of verses. Guess what? I always find an answer to my situation while going through that list. My stress falls away as a verse teaches me what to do about the situation or how to feel about it.

Follow my memorization tips and you, too, can share in the benefits of God's Word.

1. Handwrite the verse five times at one sitting.

2. Recite the verse aloud for five times at one sitting. It helps for you to hear your own voice declare God's truths. You listen to yourself all the time--now say the things God wants you to say to yourself.

3. Carry out number one and two for about a week. Make sure not to lose them by reciting them at night when you lay down to sleep, while driving to work, doing laundry, etc.

4. Feel free to add more than 20!

5. God won't mind if you personalize the verses by changing we, us, them to me, mine and myself. The goal of the bible is to change your life.

THE HEALING LIFE

Chapter Four

It is everyone's dream to live a healthy life. We go to doctors, holistic practitioners and counselors. We take pills, wear patches and apply creams. We read self-help books, watch TV doctors and research symptoms on the internet. We are counseled by our friends, magazines and hairdressers. We go to spas, join gyms and even attend life classes at church. It is clear that we put a lot of effort into the chase of the healthy life dream.

The healthy life is characterized by being sound in body, mind and spirit. To me, the word "sound" is one of those words I readily accept but really can't pin down the meaning of. So I looked it up. "Sound" means to exhibit normal health, to be solid, or whole, and stable, or steady in purpose. So a normal life means to be solid and stable physically, mentally and spiritually.

At what point can we declare that we have reached normal health? You can declare success in achieving healthy living if you feel stable, good and are growing toward new goals--in all three areas of your life--physically, mentally and spiritually. A life that isn't growing becomes stale, stagnant and diseased--in all three areas. The question is: Do you want to feel stable, good and growing toward new goals in all three areas?

The actions described in the first paragraph of this chapter suggests that we believe a healthy life is obtainable. Our chase proves that we are willing to put in effort to have it. It proves that we are sick and tired of being unsettled, disturbed and inactive.

So why is it that we've been unable to achieve the coveted healthy life from our many efforts? Our efforts obviously aren't working? So what's left for us to do? Our searches have led us to seek help from many humans, books and feel-good experiences. These aids can be good, but they are not the proper help that we need.

Consider the advice from Proverbs 3:7-8 (NCV): "Don't depend on your own wisdom. Respect the Lord and refuse to do wrong. Then your body will be healthy, and your bones will be strong." The author of this Proverb is declaring that good health comes from respecting God, our creator, and doing what he says to do and refusing to do what he says to refuse to do. Put aside human wisdom and accept God's wisdom. His wisdom is found in the Bible. It's sad that we have made our aspiration of good health such a hard goal. Good health and wholeness is so easy to obtain. Listen to Proverbs 4:21-22 (NCV): "Don't ever forget my words; keep them always in mind. They are the key to life for those who find them; they bring health to the whole body." The secret is out! Your bible is the medicine chest. Holy Spirit is your counselor. Meditation and memorization is the feel-good experience.

Don't shut me down just yet. I know it's hard to believe that words can change your life. I understand your skepticism. This chapter gives me a chance to explain how words can change your situation.

Verse 21 tells us where health starts. Go back and read it again. Have you figured out the starting point? It's in the mind. Verse 23 (GNT) explains why it's important to keep God's good words in your mind: "Be careful how you think; your life is shaped by your thoughts." We can conclude that good health starts in the mind, but what if our minds are unhealthy?

The Healed Mind

Did you know that your mind can be healed just like any other part of the body? Consider the great lengths the body goes through to heal a broken bone, a laceration in the skin, an invading infection. So, too, our minds can be healed, we just don't give much thought about it. You could say that the mind heals the mind. It takes a conscious effort (or controlled thought) to change the factors in the mind. In fact, God created the mind to be able to heal itself. God shares this wonderful healing secret in Romans 12:2 (NLT): "Don't copy the behavior and customs of this world, but let God transform you into a new person by changing the way you think. Then you will know what God wants you to do and you will know how good and pleasing and perfect his will really is."

Notice that there are two sources of influence to the mind. The most common source is the world. The world can be broken down in a few categories: Satan, other humans and self. The other less popular source is God. God's source is found in the bible and Holy Spirit. Romans 12:2 reveals that you will live a good, pleasing and perfect life if you change your thinking to God's thinking. And note that you'll know what God wants you to do--hence, your purpose for being on this earth.

Understand?

We don't take the promises found in God's word seriously. We humans tend to think that something is bad if we don't understand it. We trust what we already know. So why aren't we willing to expand the information in our minds? I want to challenge you to learn a new thing. Get to know God for who he is. He's much bigger and more powerful than you think. According to Ephesians 3:20 (NCV) he wants to empower us beyond our understanding: "With God's power working in us, God can do much, much more than anything we can ask or imagine." Just ask him to help you to know him better.

The Real Me

Most of my life I have lived as a painfully shy person. I thought I was invisible. I felt alone even when I was around family members. I was living an unhealthy life, mentally and spiritually. That led to a deflated physical life. But one thing kept me from completely withering away. My Salvation! I was secure in the fact that Jesus died for me and that God is my Father. But what I lacked was the feeling of being rescued from loneliness and invisibility.

I was still plagued with the lower standards of living when I began my writing career. I realized I had areas that needed to be healed before I could be of good use to Father. One morning I asked God to father me. Within an hour, he answered that request. I was looking up some words in the dictionary. I was surprised when I came across a form of my name. Look at what Father told me. "Wynd:" to wind, proceed, go. "Wyn" or "Wynn" is a variation of wen. "Wen" means joy and winsome. Winsome means pleasing and engaging and cheerful. Father told me that I am not the shy, lonely and invisible person that I had come to accept. He said that I am an energetic, on-the-go type person, engaging in relationships and happy with the life he has given me.

A Letter from God

"Dear children, I know that you have suffered traumatic experiences in your lives, most of them out of your control. Your experiences vary in range from horrific to hurtful, from physical and sexual to mental abuse. Pain, images and hurtful words are seared on your minds. You cannot seem to separate yourselves from the events.

Child, who would you be today if you hadn't been traumatized? My precious child, you would still be the same you. My goal is for you to move beyond that moment in time and allow it to give purpose to your life. You are probably willing to admit that you can get passed the actual experience, however, the thoughts you have of yourself is keeping you prisoner. Satan knew you would take the event as a sign that you are trash, unlovable, unacceptable and of no worth. The truth is: you don't belong to Satan. You are still my creation. I love you and accept you. You are of great worth because I created you!!

Now my child, I want you to turn to me and receive my love, acceptance and worth. Grieve over the past and forgive the human (s) who hurt you. Turn the consequences of the inflictor over to me. I will make sure that justice is served. But I ask you to go a step further and be willing to love your inflictor as I do. I will help you to love that person. I want the same results for the one who hurt you as I do for you. My goal is for everyone to turn to me and live healthy lives. Love you dearly and deeply, Holy Dad."

Bad Memory, Bad Behavior

I am asking for your permission to speak about a sensitive subject. Memories can be good and they can be disturbing. It would seem that memories are beyond our control. Memories shape our lives. Passions are catapulted from them. Some of them drive us into isolation and depression. It would help us to know what memories are and how they work. Memories are visual mental episodes of past experiences that are stored deep in the mind. We replay these episodes over and over. We relive the pain each time we rerun them. Sometimes the memories pop up of no fault of our own. A scent, a word, a sound can trigger the event. But what can we do about these life-altering mental episodes?

Let's look at memory from a different angle. A memory tells a one-sided story. Would we react to the mental episode differently if we knew all the facts surrounding the event? Take note that a bad memory puts you in a bad mood causing you to behave badly. I think of sin when I hear the words "bad behavior." And sin separates us from a close relationship with Father. Do you agree that a bad memory does the same thing? See if the words spoken in Romans 8:2 (MSG) sound like a bad memory: "The Spirit of life in Christ, like a strong wind, has magnificently cleared the air, freeing you from a fated lifetime of brutal tyranny at the hands of sin and death." Bad memories seem to last a lifetime and are brutal. Yet, turning your life over to Christ- mind, memories, everything, heals us from the torture.

Do you want to stop living a tortured life from bad memories? 1 Peter 2:24 (NCV) tells us what we have to stop doing and what we have to start doing: "Christ carried our sins in his body on the cross so we would stop living for sin and start living for what is right. And you are healed because of his wounds." The sensitive truth is that when we focus on the bad memories we behave badly. The focus stays constant for long periods of time or occurs frequently or both. The things we focus on become our gods. Since we've learned that memories are located in the deep mind, we can be certain that memories can be healed. Ask Father to heal your memories--he healed mine!

Mental Reality

Satan is an excellent illusionist! Acting under the influence of sin/memory/fear is like putting your hands over your eyes and imagining things instead of experiencing reality. Satan tricks you into his schemes just by shifting your attention away from God through your thoughts and expectations. We have a tendency to be disillusioned by others comments and by what we think they mean by them. Romans 8:6 (NCV) warns us of this: "If people's thinking is controlled by the sinful self, there is death. But if their thinking is controlled by the Spirit, there is life and peace." We get caught up in people's words rather than God's words. I don't understand why we do this. God created us and loves us. People hurt us and don't show love to us. The hurtful people aren't interested in us living a healthy life or they would speak helpful things to us. God wants us to live good lives and he offers helpful advice.

At times, we find ourselves hostages to bad thoughts and memories. There is a mental tool you can use to pull yourself out of the captor's hands and into the present reality. Make yourself aware of the things around you: where are you, what are you doing, who are you with? The present moment, the present task and the person who is in your present are meant to be enjoyed.

Alive and Working

Thoughts are mental words. Mental words are like shoes. Ill-fitting shoes produce pain. The pain causes you to sit as often as possible. You experience no enjoyment in the activity. Painful feet make you grouchy. Your feet swell and reddened areas appear at the pressure points. However, proper fitting shoes are barely noticed. They become a foundation of comfort so your feet can transport you to places to do things. You enjoy the activities of the day. You accomplish tasks and plan for more. Mental words fit just like shoes.

One of my core 20 memory verses is Hebrews 4:12 (NCV): "God's word is alive and working and is sharper than a double-edged sword. It cuts all the way into us, where the soul and the spirit are joined, to the center of our joints and bones. And it judges the thoughts and feelings in our hearts." I shared with you in the last chapter how memorizing God's words have changed my life--thus proving that God's word is alive and working. So, if his words are alive and working why wouldn't our mental words also be alive and working? The experience I had with bible memorization proves that his word changed my thoughts, my beliefs and my emotions. My life now has a foundation of comfort that allows me to go out and enjoy the activities of my day.

Mental Path

Thoughts become habits. Repeated thoughts form well-worn paths of signals in the brain. It's important to know that our minds/thoughts control the brain. These well-worn paths of signal become natural or second nature. But that doesn't mean they become permanent. These paths can be changed. Fear is a mental bully. It wants you to travel down its path--but you don't have to. Fear seems loud and overpowering. What fear doesn't want you to know is that it is an emotion and an emotion is changed by a thought. Anger is also a bully, is loud, and overpowering, but, anger is also an emotion that can be changed by a thought.

The brain is a one-track organ. It travels in only one direction (or path) at a time. The path is negative or positive, good or bad. Jesus speaks of a path he wants you to take in Matthew 7:13-14 (GNT): "Go in through the narrow gate, because the gate to hell is wide and the road that leads to it is easy, and there are many who travel it. But the gate to life is narrow and the way that leads to it is hard and there are few people who find it." The first paragraph of this chapter alludes to the wrong paths that we humans take in order to find a healthy life. The right path isn't popular. I'm afraid people put hands over their eyes and refuse to look for the right path.

The wrong mental path leads to all sorts of chaotic mind problems. Listen to James 1:8 (AMP) and see if you personally suffer from these mind distortions: "[For being as he is] a man of two minds (hesitating, dubious, irresolute), [he is] unstable and unreliable and uncertain about everything [he thinks, feels, and decides]." Now listen to James 1:7 (GNT): "If you act like that, unable to make up your mind and undecided in all you do, you must not think that you will receive anything from the Lord." Did you notice that the bad mental path is not on God's path? You can't even blame God for the bad stuff happening in your life caused by a bad mental path.

Do you want a good life? Then choose God's good path--- that's what James 4:8 (GWT) says: "Come close to God, and he will come close to you. Clean up your lives, you sinners, and clear your minds, you doubters." Just imagine the kind of life you can have by eliminating doubt! An eye-opening truth is that the opposite of doubt is confidence. God designed you to feel his confidence! Isn't that wonderful?!

Stand Up Mentally

Have you ever had a life change that resulted in you wanting to drop some bad-influencing friends? You worried about how to go about dropping them but discovered that they dropped you when your lifestyle no longer fit theirs. Your paths were not going in the same direction. The same is true of the influence of Satan as told in James 4:7 (NCV): "So give yourselves completely to God. Stand against the devil, and the devil will run from you."

Completely means completely--all of your life. That means your belief life, thought life, emotional life and physical life. When you give your total life to God your old friends (fear, anger, jealousy, and doubt) will be traveling in the opposite direction. Make a decision right now to mentally stand up, turn around and travel God's path.

Mental Tools

Your daily life includes health care activities. Such activities include: hair care, teeth care, energy care (from food and beverage), and clothing care. Why not include mental care? Choose an effective time of day (are you a morning or night person?) to work on your mental health. Journaling is an excellent way. You can write out all of your grievances and talk to God about them. Writing down your thoughts helps you to identify problem areas. One huge benefit I have from doing this is I have the chance to hash out my problems to God before Sunday. Sundays have turned out to be free worship days. I don't go to church expecting to find comfort. My comfort has already been met at home. Instead, I go to church expecting to enjoy God. That was a benefit I hadn't thought of before--one of those beyond-my-imagination benefits that God promises us. And I might add-a benefit I don't want to lose!

I discovered another tool while listening to an interview on Joyce Meyer's show. She was interviewing Dr. Caroline Leaf, a Christian neuroscientist. She shared that handwriting God's word once a day for 21 days would rewire the brain. I quickly embraced the concept but I took it a step further. I developed a series of 21-day journal notes, a tool I continue to use when needed. The note is only a paragraph long. I use a sentence or two describing my distress over a problem area. You can look at this part as a confession to God. I continue the note with a bible verse that counteracts the problem. I claim victory as stated by the bible verse. I always end with a word of thanks to God. This tool completely changed my mental life.

I remember the first months I employed this technique. I felt such deep comfort and new energy while writing these notes. I enjoyed my time so much that I took my notebook with me on vacation. I found a quiet spot in the lobby by the fireplace and wrote out my daily note. 21 days seems to work well for me but I have since heard Dr. Leaf say that some folks need more days added. It makes sense because we all learn in different ways and in different time frames. A wonderful benefit is that you feel a change of attitude by day four but a complete rewiring comes from a full 21 days (or the amount you are wired for). She stressed the need to handwrite instead of typing them on the computer. I later learned from research that the movement of the fingers used while handwriting releases a massive amount of learning from the brain. That explains what Proverbs 7:3 (NIRV) means: "Tie them on your fingers. Write them on the tablets of your heart." This verse was referring to obeying his words.

Christmas Year Round

Take your child-self and travel back in time to any Christmas Eve Night. You were so excited. The next day was even more exciting. You squealed with delight as you ripped tons of Christmas paper from the packages. Isn't it funny that we forget about grudges, distresses, and ill feelings during this special season? Good will flows all over the place and is felt by almost everyone.

The exciting thing is that Jesus provides that kind of joy and good-will all year long, not just on his birthday. It is felt when our mental lives are healed. An example is that of enjoying life even though the weather is stormy. You find yourself thanking God for really nothing in general--or everything in general. I was not the type to lift my hands up in worship at church--until my mental life was healed.

But I have to give you a warning. Healing is not a dramatic thing. You will notice it by accident. You'll discover healing when you react in a different way to a difficult situation than you would have reacted in the past. You may even find the peacefulness of your healed life a bit boring. That's because you are used to mental chaos. But don't worry, once you get used to the new way of life other things will pop up. Gifts and talents will appear that were stifled before. Passion and purpose will give your life new pizzazz. You will feel closeness to God that you will never want to lose. You will indeed enjoy Christmas excitement year round.

Butterfly Life

The springtime season is full of new-life joys. Flowers appear. Birds lay eggs. Grass becomes green. Leaves spread out on the branches. But the most relaxing feature of spring is that of the butterfly. Butterflies gracefully fly around. They enjoy soaking up the warm sun while sitting on a flower petal. They come in all shapes and sizes and colors. You probably knew all of that, but did you know that butterfly is an ancient Greek word meaning soul and mind? I think God meant for butterflies to give us a visual picture of our mental selves.

If you recall, the butterfly starts out as a caterpillar in a dark cocoon. We, too, spend time in dark places. While in the cocoon, it digests itself. Sounds a lot like God asking us to give up ourselves to him. Once the process has been completed, a beautiful, graceful butterfly emerges. That's what I feel like since being transformed by God's word! Friend, dare to allow God to transform you into a beautiful butterfly by changing the way you think!!

THE ENGAGED LIFE

Chapter Five

One Tuesday afternoon I invited my first lady (pastor's wife) to my home for a lunch date. As it turned out, it was a snowy day. I greatly appreciate that she braved the weather for some friendship time with me. I served a home-cooked meal, she provided wonderful company and we both enjoyed friendly conversation. We learned some new things about each other that day.

I was excited to share with her a bible study I had written. It is essentially a shorter version of this book. I have handed this study out to a few ladies hoping to help them find new life as I have.

I shared with my first lady that I became a believer in Jesus Christ at age 15. I also revealed that I didn't become a serious follower until my middle years. You may be asking what the difference is. Read on and you'll find out.

My middle years started out intense and stressful. I found myself working long hours, driving a long commute and not spending enough time with my family. Oh, I forgot to tell you that I wasn't spending any personal time with God. But something small changed everything.

You can imagine the chaos of my mind with all the busyness in my life. My mind was a crowded and noisy place. It's a wonder that I heard the quiet voice asking me to read the bible and pray. I surprised myself when I answered "ok." I told God that I had precious little time to spare but I was willing to give him 15 minutes a day. Some of you seasoned Christians may be unhappy with my 15-minute promise but I'll share with you later how I know he was ok with my offer.

I set the alarm on the clock to wake me up at 4:45 A.M. I got up and read the bible for 7 1/2 minutes and prayed for the other 7 1/2 minutes. I enjoyed our time together more than I had expected. During those small increments of time, Father God advised me on how to deal with things that I was experiencing. It was amazing how the portion of scripture I was reading addressed those areas. Father blessed those few precious moments I gave him.

I told my first lady that I became hooked on Jesus from that 15-minute promise. My husband's interpretation of "being hooked" is "being sold out for Christ." As the word "hook" suggests, I was ensnared by the new relationship.

The funny thing is I had been serving God prior to the quiet invitation. I sang in the choir, taught Sunday School classes, took a mission trip to Romania, taught a bible study at work and supported my husband's ministry. It sounds as if I were already hooked on Jesus, doesn't it?

The 15 minutes of time spent with Father were meaningful to me and him. How do I know this? If I were him, I would be impressed with the willingness to sacrifice 15 precious minutes of sleep. I'm sure he appreciated that my first waking moments were devoted to hearing from him. He engaged me first with the quiet invitation and I engaged with him through conversation and listening. We shared, we bonded and we befriended each other, much like the lunch date I had with my first lady.

My love for him grew by keeping company with him. Ephesians 5:2a (MSG) confirms how the relationship grew: "Mostly what God does is love you. Keep company with Him and learn a life of love." Spending time serving God is not enough to qualify as a relationship. Time spent conversing and listening to God grows a strong, healthy relationship between the two of you.

What God wants from you is a relationship with him, one-on-one. Why are we so blinded to his wishes? You could say there is a relationship battle waging inside of us. You might be surprised to find out who the battle is with. Winning half a battle is admitting the truth of any situation. The truth is, "we" are the opposing army. Self wants to keep its own routine. How many of you would be willing to get up at 4:45 a.m. to spend time with Father? We like making our own rules, plans and thoughts. How many of you would give your first waking moments to God? We enjoy our independence and are reluctant to give it up. Do you have space in your life for another (the most important) relationship?

We Christians participate in activities that serve God for a variety of reasons. One of those reasons is to perform for others. We know that serving in church activities looks "Christian-like" for those who are watching us. Another reason is to satisfy our self. Self is willing to do just enough to not feel guilty. It could be that a view of the Christian life has been taught to us with a heavy emphasis on service rather than a relationship that evokes service. My relationship with Father has energized my services to him. My service is not the same as it was before.

Crisis Engagement

The only time some of us turn to him for a one-on-one conversation is when we are facing a crisis. Friend, he'll receive you in that moment of desperation, but he knows when the crisis is over, the engagement is over. It's back to the old habits and routines. The brief relationship turns out to be a selfish one, not a two-way affair. It turns into a short-term fix instead of a long-term, loyal situation.

Forms of Engagement

What word or thought comes to your mind when you hear the word "engagement?" I bet you said "marriage." That's what comes to my mind first. An engagement is a declaration to the world that you are committing yourself to another person. A wedding celebration is planned. Vows are written. The wedding vows remind me of our vows to God. Psalm 116:14 (NIV) reminds us that we, too, make a vow to God: "I will fulfill my vows to the Lord in the presence of all his people." Verse 13 reveals our declaration to the world: "I will lift up the cup of salvation and call on the name of the Lord." Salvation means we are committed to Christ for life.

You enter into the engagement of marriage when you believe you have found the right person to spend the rest of your life with. You accept salvation when you believe you have found the right savior to spend the rest of your life with.

The bible speaks of the wife submitting to the husband. James 4:7 tells us to submit to God. A lot of people cringe at the sound of the word "submit." But wait just a minute! Consider how the word "commit" (which we are ok with) compares with the word "submit." Submit means to cease resistance. Commit means to connect and trust. Now add love and loyalty to either of the two words. Love and loyalty softens our attitudes toward them. If you don't love the one you are engaged to then you won't willingly submit to them.

Seriously Engaged

I use the phrase "follow the love" quite often to point to the reason why people do what they do. People surrender to love all the time. Some examples are: love of money, love of a mate, love of clothes. We surrender to whatever we love because it gives us a good feeling. We enjoy the thing we love.

I am going to boldly say that there was a time when you didn't love "the thing" you now love. You didn't love it until you experienced it. The same thought applies to God. We won't love him unless we experience him. That means choosing to spend time with him, conversing and listening to him. It means surrendering to the Bible by reading it, studying it, memorizing his words and even loving the truths found in it. I like to think of the Bible as God's mind in the form of words.

Unfortunately, a lot of us Christians read the bible as if it's a book of fiction, a good read, but not applicable to our lives. 2 Timothy 4:3-4 (NLT) describes this type of attitude: "For a time is coming when people will no longer listen to sound and wholesome teaching. They will follow their own desires and will look for teachers who will tell them whatever their itching ears want to hear. They will reject the truth and chase after myths." A sad truth is we tend to read his promises and duly note them. We don't get hooked by his promises because we don't believe them. Matthew 13:13b (GWT) sums it up: "They hear, but they don't listen. They don't even try to understand." Friend, I've been the one who read it but didn't hear it because I didn't believe it. I've also been the one who read it, heard it and believed it. It happened when I submitted and committed to him. That's when I fell more in love and loyalty.

42

A biblical look at seriousness is found in Jeremiah 29:13a (MSG): "When you come looking for me, you'll find me, yes, when you get serious about finding me and want it more than anything else." I proved my seriousness to God when I alarmed my clock for 4:45 a.m. and spent the first 15 minutes of my day with him.

More seriousness followed. I kept up my daily meeting with him faithfully. I started studying my Sunday school lessons as if looking for gold gems. I received encouragement from women speakers on TV. Joyce Meyer and Beth Moore were especially helpful. I felt God speaking to me through them concerning emotional issues. I felt new energy as a result of my seriousness.

The Engaged Mind

You could say I was fully engaged to God. I was attracted to his influence over my life. I loved my God experience. 1 Peter 4:2 (NIRV) described my state of mind: "As a result, they don't live the rest of their earthly life for evil human desires. Instead, they live to do what God wants." My desires changed. I wanted what God wanted. And I didn't have to force myself to change my wants to his wants. It just happened.

The feeling of "want" is a powerful feeling. "Want" is another word for the word "will." If you recall from Chapter Two, The Enriched Life, the will is located in the mind. We do only what we want or will ourselves to do. The "want" or "will" is a self-convincer. It persuades us to do what it wants to do because we feel enjoyment from the activity. But what happens when our want and will clash with God's want and will?

Tension builds between a married couple. It causes mental and emotional strain. The two feel they can no longer coexist so they get divorced. Disloyalty is the main cause for divorces. It may be disloyalty with finances, attention, or trustworthiness. James 1:6 (NLT) describes how disloyalty causes turmoil: "But when you ask him, be sure that your faith is in God alone. Do not waver, for a person with divided loyalty is as unsettled as a wave of the sea that is blown and tossed by the wind." Loyalty is a "willed" act. It starts in the mind where a person wills himself\herself to stay true to the vows made to the other party.

Our loyalty to God fluctuates much like it does for a married couple. Love is stolen from one spouse and given to another person. The marriage suffers. It becomes unhealthy. You, too, become unhealthy when you are disloyal to God. James 1:8 (NLT) tells how you will be affected: "Their loyalty is divided between God and the world, and they are unstable in everything they do." Have you considered that your messed up life is due to your unfaithfulness to him and his teachings?

You may be wondering how it is that you can give your love for God away? 1 John 2:15-16 (NCV) reveals how it is possible: "Do not love the world or the things in the world. If you love the world, the love of the Father is not in you. These are the ways of the world: wanting to please our sinful selves, wanting the sinful things we see and being too proud of what we have. None of these come from the Father, but all of them are from the world." Did you notice the word "wanting?" You give your God-love away when you want things that are opposite to what God wants.

Jesus (husband of the church) wants to reconcile with you. He has forgiven your unfaithfulness. Are you willing to bring your love back to God? Galatians 5:24-25 (NCV) encourages reconciliation: "Those who belong to Christ Jesus have crucified their own sinful selves. They have given up their old selfish feelings and the evil things they wanted to do. We get our new life from the Spirit, so we should follow the Spirit." And Ephesians 4:23-24 (GWT) relates the reconciliation to the mind: "However, you were taught to have a new attitude. You were also taught to become a new person created to be like God, truly righteous and holy." Note that the mind is the part of us that receives teaching.

So, if you want your messy, crazy life cleaned up and organized--then love God, be loyal to him, receive his teachings and enjoy the benefits. According to Ephesians 4:23-24, being like God, righteous and holy, can be taught and caught in the mind, making you more like Jesus. Learn his ways so that you can have a good, clear mind to receive larger amounts of his teachings.

James 1:8 (GWT) teaches: "A person who has doubts is thinking about different things at the same time and can't make up his mind about anything." Weigh out the thought of this verse. It means that doubt and certainty (faith) in the mind at the same time produces confusion. Do you remember that the brain is a one-track organ? Imagine the fight between doubt and faith over the path in the brain. Brain drain. Brain fog. Confusion. These mind conditions are miserable.

Enjoying the Engaged Life

Mental wholeness is within your grasp--it's within your mind's grasp. I find this extremely exciting! So many of us suffer from mental instability and chaos. Isaiah 26:3 (MSG) encourages us to not give up: "People with their minds set on you, you keep completely whole, steady on their feet, because they keep at it and don't quit."

Bear with me as I share a couple of lengthy verses with you. Notice the positive path in Philippians 4:8 (MSG): "Summing it all up, friends, I'd say you'll do best by filling your minds and meditating on things true, noble, reputable, authentic, compelling, gracious--the best, not the worst; the beautiful, not the ugly; things to praise, not things to curse." Friend, imagine a life where the mind is filled with good, truthful things, beautiful and genuine. It makes for an excellent life. God is telling you he wants this for you. Verse 9 has more advise: "Put into practice what you learned from me, what you heard and saw and realized. Do that, and God, who makes everything work together, will work you into his most excellent harmonies." "Excellent harmonies" describes how he wants your mind to be. Father tells us, though, that we have to practice thinking the things he teaches us in order to have our minds healed. You can do it! He will help you!

New Engagements

I diligently worked as a nurse for 27 years. I enjoyed serving my patients, coworkers, and employers. However, the life of a nurse can be stressful. I see all of you nurses nodding you heads. I day dreamed of quitting and becoming an interior decorator. However, finances kept me a prisoner in a stressful situation.

During this high-stressed time of my life, I turned to my cheerleaders on TV--Joyce Meyer and Beth Moore. I was drawn to what they were doing. I thought to myself "can I be a bible teacher, too?" I decided to tell God that I wanted to work for him. I didn't know exactly what kind of job God was going to give me but I knew I would enjoy it. I don't know how I knew I would enjoy it, but I did.

God knows me well. He knew I would never feel comfortable quitting my job. In 2008, the job market declined. Mine, of course, was stable, but Keevin's (my husband) was not. It was a shaky time. And then something happened that changed my career path. The oil pump on my car exploded. We could not afford to have it repaired. So I no longer had a personal vehicle. I had no transportation for work. We ended up moving back to Murfreesboro, TN where Keevin could find good, steady work that would support us.

We lived in our camper for about seven months while we recovered from the financial setback. It was during that time that I began my writing career. I took my cue from my cheerleaders on TV and began writing a bible study. Thus, my new employer was God. I just started writing about things that were personal to me and things he showed me about my problem areas. One thing I developed while in the camper was my writing style. I call it "Wynndy language." I really love my style of writing and enjoy the gift God has given me.

After seven months in the camper, we moved into the perfect size home along with our children and grandchildren. I enjoyed reconnecting with them and sharing space with them. We celebrated birthdays and holidays. Happy memories were made in that home.

But other things were created there. It was in that home that I wrote my first real bible study. It was in that home that God inspired my 21-day journal notes. It was in that home that I received mental health and wholeness.

I didn't have much money. I still didn't have a personal vehicle. But I had a new mental life and a job working for the best boss ever. I had a new gift of writing, family closeness and new purpose for my life. I was the happiest I had ever been. It's funny as I think back on that time that I was never mad about losing my car or my nursing career. That's the way life happens when one is seriously engaged with God.

Other Engagements

Little did I know while we were living in that house that my husband, Keevin, was having a serious conversation with God. He talked to God for a year before sharing his new engagement with me.

His feelings of restlessness and dissatisfaction led him to talk to God. God called him to ministry early in our marriage, so he, too, was supposed to be working for God. He told God that he was now serious about his ministry. Like me, he didn't have a clear understanding of what he was supposed to be doing. So Keevin told God: "Wherever, whatever, and whenever". Amazingly, God gave him several confirmations of a destination (the wherever). Keevin wanted to be completely confident that he was hearing God correctly, so he asked for more signs. God gave him more signs in unusual places pointing to Boone, NC. Keevin now knew the destination but was unsure of the "whatever."

He was so afraid to tell me about his new engagement, but I wasn't afraid to receive it. I recalled earlier in our marriage when he popped a question to me while on vacation. "What would you think if God was calling me to preach?" I replied: "I wouldn't be surprised." We are both from families of God communicators, and pastors. In fact, I had a feeling (a feeling that God had put in me) that I would marry a preacher--that's why I wasn't surprised. My husband has proven that he has a great gift of being able to share Jesus' Good News.

We are still pursuing God's call. As usual, we are not the usual. We feel God is leading us to minister to a different set of folks. We have compassion towards people who have been hurt or misunderstood by the church. We have a passion to see people of all walks in life receive salvation--no matter what their past or present life is. We welcome all black sheep and misfits into Jesus' care. We want everyone (and so does God) to experience new life and good life.

John 1:12 (AMP) tells us that all are welcome: "But to as many as did receive and welcome Him, He gave the authority (power, privilege, right) to become the children of God, that is, to those who believe in (adhere to, trust in, and rely on) His name." Friend, if you feel like an outsider, invisible or troubled, He welcomes you into his family. Verse 13 (TLB) explains how you, a misfit, can become his child: "All those who believe this are reborn!--not a physical rebirth resulting from human passion or plan--but from the will of God." Father God wants to be your new Daddy! He doesn't see you as an outsider or a troublemaker. He sees you as belonging to him and fitting into his big loving family.

Fear of Engagement

Now, don't let our unusual calling scare you away from your calling. Every Christian has a purpose from God. He calls all of us, even the misfits, to live a life that displays him. You

47

understandably can't envision your new life and purpose because it looks nothing like you have experienced before. Make that thought ok within yourself. Consider the advice in Galatians 5:16 (AMP) and take it a small step at a time: "But I say, walk and live [habitually] in the [Holy] Spirit [responsive to and controlled and guided by the Spirit]; then you will certainly not gratify the cravings and desires of the flesh (of human nature without God)." This verse suggests creating a new thinking pattern, a new path of living. Proverbs 3:6 (MSG) explains how you can stay on God's path: "Listen for God's voice in everything you do, everywhere you go; He's the one who will keep you on track."

Fear suggests danger. Change is not meant to be a fearful event but that's how we envision it. Satan uses his trickery of disillusionment to stop you--dead in your tracks. You may feel a closeness to your lifestyle, whether you are a misfit, outsider or troubled person. This lifestyle has served you in an odd way. It has given you an identity. Identity and purpose hold hands. You feel loyal to your lifestyle because it has made you feel like somebody with a voice. You have championed your way of living and are proud of it. Why give it up if it seems so wonderful? Ask yourself these two questions: "Could another type of life be more wonderful? Why destine myself to a mediocre type experience?"

There are two ways to face the danger of change: fear or confidence. Guess which one overcomes danger? It isn't fear. Fear is given to us by Satan. God gives us confidence. Satan hates you. God loves you. Which one do you want to receive gifts from?

A confident way to face change is to consider the pros and cons of the new life and compare it to the old life. You've been loyal to the old life because of the pros, but have you considered the cons. Have you weighed the differences between the pros and cons? You might discover that you bought into a lifestyle without confronting all the facts about it. That's a special trick of Satan's.

James 1:12 (MSG) champions you to face a change confidently: "Anyone who meets a testing challenge head-on and manages to stick it out is mighty fortunate. For such persons loyally in love with God, the reward is life and more life." You can exchange the misfit, troubled life for one that is confident and courageous. Wouldn't you rather be known as a person full of life and enjoying every minute of it?

Vow to Engage

The last step of engagement is to declare your love and loyalty to God. It is appropriate for you to vow a life of faithfulness and attention to Jesus. He is the groom of the church and deserves your love. Your life choice will reward you with the bliss of paradise. Take note of what 1 Peter 1:13 (GWT) says: "Therefore, your minds must be clear and ready for action. Place your confidence completely in what God's kindness will bring you when Jesus Christ appears again."

As you exchange vows (from old life to new life) remind yourself that you are no longer a caterpillar. You have emerged a graceful and beautiful butterfly!

THE TREE OF LIFE

Chapter Six

I met with a group of women one Saturday evening. The purpose of our meeting was to discuss a new women's ministry idea. We enjoyed a meal of home cooked lasagna as well as friendly conversation. A work of art caught my eye as we sat at the dining room table. Our host had painted a tree of life on a wall. It was a beautiful site, visually and emotionally. Each member was given importance with their name on a branch of the tree.

Genealogy has been a fascination of mine. It started back in the 70's when Aunt Dean researched the Parker family history. The information was interesting and intriguing. It was as if a door had been opened to a closet filled with reasons and answers as to how our family had been shaped. And you might guess, Aunt Dean worked long and hard to obtain our precious identity because this was pre-internet time.

Keevin's Uncle Benny presented family information at a Wilson family reunion a few years ago. Both the Wilson and Parker families have some unique characters to boast about. There are also some shady ones found in both. The good and the bad. Every family has that in common. Look at the first family, Adam and Eve. You can find good and bad in their accounts.

Have you ever projected your thoughts into future generations and considered how your life account might affect family members to come? I would be thrilled if my life story could encourage a great, great niece or nephew to live the new life. Wouldn't it be awesome to steer a young person, yet to be born, in the right direction just by you living a good life now? Listen to this odd fact--you can have a relationship of sorts with someone you won't physically meet. Will anyone thank you for inspiring them to do good things when you meet them in heaven?

The Tree of Life is a picture (literally and figuratively) of the family. Familial relationships consist of blended personalities that are connected by birth, adoption or marriage. All of us are born to our biological parents. Some are raised and influenced by the birth parents. Others are chosen to grow up in an adopted family. In the case of adoption, the child faces difficulty of not being accepted into the birth family and the receiving family has had difficulty having a child of their own to love. I think God uses adoption as one of those "turn a bad thing into a good thing" situation. Marriage adds another dimension of personalities and influence. The family legacy provides a foundation for your life. It could be a solid foundation or a shaky one.

What did God have in mind when he created us humans? Genesis 1:26 (TLB) begins to answer our question: "Then God said, 'Let us make a man--someone like ourselves, to be the master of all life upon the earth and in the skies and in the seas.'" And verse 28a (NIRV) continues: "God blessed them. He said to them, 'Have children so that there will be many of you. Fill the earth and bring it under your control.'" The answer is he created us for relationships. The first relationship is with Him, Jesus, and Holy Spirit. The second relationship is with the family. And more relationships extend outside the family circle.

Follow the family line with me. God was Adam and Eve's daddy. He becomes our daddy when we join the God family. He adopts us and cares for us just like he did for the first son and daughter. He placed Adam and Eve in a beautiful home, the Garden of Eden. Even though we don't live in the Garden of Eden, this earth is still extremely beautiful. Let's visit Adam and Eve in the Garden. Genesis 2:8-9 (NLT): 'Then the Lord God planted a garden in Eden in the east, and there He placed the man he had made. The Lord God make all sorts of trees grow up from the ground--trees that were beautiful and that produce delicious fruit. In the middle of the garden he placed the Tree of Life and the Tree of the Knowledge of Good and Evil."

The family was meant to grow and be enhanced in the Garden. Even though there were many beautiful trees bearing delicious fruit, two other trees stood tall and prominent. These two trees are the key to the health of the family life. Proverbs 3:18 (NLT) takes a look up into one of the trees: "Wisdom is a tree of life to those who embrace her; happy are those who hold her tightly." And Genesis 2:17 (NIRV) looks up into the other tree: "But you must not eat the fruit of the tree of the knowledge of good and evil. If you do, you can be sure that you will die." There they are, side by side, representing a test of loyalty and love.

Adam and Eve chose to break off their love and loyalty to God when they ate from the Tree of the Knowledge of Good and Evil. Immediately they realized, "Oh, no! I've made a terrible mistake." Life changed, their home changed, family values changed. Would things ever get back to normal for them, for us? The answer is YES! John 14:6 (Voice) explains: "Jesus: I am the path, the truth, and the energy of life. No one comes to the Father except through Me." Jesus reconnects us back to Daddy. He repairs the brokenness of our family ties and opens up dialogue with the One who loves us and cares for us.

Tree of Life Trivia

Question number one: Where did the concept of the tree of life as a family tree originate?

Answer: Pat yourself on the back if you answered "the bible." Isaiah 11:1 (NCV) plainly tells us: "A new branch will grow from the stump of a tree; so a new king will come from the family of Jesse." Verse 2 (Voice) clarifies that this king is not King David but someone else to follow: "And this child from David's line, the Spirit of the Eternal One will alight and rest. By the Spirit of wisdom and discernment, He will shine like the dew. By the Spirit of counsel and strength he will judge fairly and act courageously." "The Spirit" implies that he is Jesus, God and Spirit, not the human David. Did the word "wisdom" jump out at you? Even though the Tree of the Knowledge of Good and Evil implies knowledge, real wisdom comes from the Tree of Life.

Question number two: Jesus is perfect. Was Jesus' family tree filled with perfect people?

Answer: High-five someone if you answered "no." Jesus'

genealogy is full of interesting people with equally intriguing stories. His family line encourages us and steers us to better lives.

Question number three: Since Jesus is "The King of the Jews" was his family lineage that of Jewish royalty?

Answer: Get up and do the happy dance if you answered "no." Jesus' lineage is a mixture of cultures and nationalities and it didn't alter his supremeness one bit!

Find Yourself in Jesus' Family Tree

Regardless of nationality or religion, male dominance was common in the Middle East back then and still is today. Females didn't fair too well. For that reason, Jewish genealogies did not record female members. It was as if females didn't exist. They must have felt invisible and voiceless.

Then Jesus was born. His life changed attitudes. His death buried the unfairness of treatment so commonly practiced. His resurrection raised new life and new values to all who would believe. His genealogy features and records women who were important to his story. Men and women can gleam hope and change through the lives of those names in this very important list. I'm going to feature the women, as he did, because of the very unusual nature of them being recognized. I believe you can relate to one or more of these fine ladies and be energized to live your new life.

Meet Tamar. You can relate to her if you've looked for love in all the wrong places. She was not a Jew. Her sad story is that she was given in marriage to an evil man of the Jewish nationality and faith. He was so evil that God killed him. The Jewish law required that the father-n-law give the widow the next son in line in order to bear an heir for the deceased son. The next son was just as wicked as the first. He had sexual relations with her but stopped short of allowing her to become pregnant. God killed the second son also. Judah, the father-n-law, feared he would lose his third son should he give him to Tamar. Judah sent Tamar back to her father's home to live as a widow. He sentenced her to a life of no inheritance or provision. The only worth a woman could attain to was that of bearing children, which she was denied. You can imagine her anger and disappointment. Sheer survival caused her to make a poor decision. Tamar disguised herself as a prostitute and approached Judah, her former father-n-law. He gladly paid for her services. As you would guess, she became pregnant and revealed it to him later on. Notice how her bad decision didn't keep her out of Jesus' lineage.

Allow me to introduce you to Rahab. Any person with a promiscuous past can bond with her. Rahab lived in the city of Jericho, which was in the land of Canaan. Canaan was promised to the children of Israel but it was filled with giant-sized, aggressive people. She provided for herself through the money she made as a prostitute. She, too, was not a Jew. Joshua and 2 other men secretly entered Jericho to check out the property. The men found themselves in a bit of danger and needed a hiding place. Rahab courageously allowed them into her home and hid them. It was a perfect situation as she had a flow of men coming and going from her home all the time. But a funny thing happened. She believed all they said about their God. Rahab was King David's great, great grandma.

Next in line is Ruth. Inappropriate sexual acts between family members can damage and almost destroy the core of a human being. It is the worst of all generational sins as it is usually passed down from one generation to the next. If this type of existence describes your life then you can be redeemed, cleaned up and made pure along with Ruth. Ruth was not a Jew. She was a Moabite. She was born as a result of incest. Incest was widely practiced in the country of Moab and was no big deal to the aggressor. I don't know the back-story as to how she came to be married to a Jewish man, but he died before they had children. Her wonderful mother-n-law introduced her to God. Note that her father-n-law also died around the time of this story. Her mother-n-law, Naomi, chose to return to her homeland. Ruth made an unusual decision to follow Naomi. She followed her in order to serve Naomi's God. She didn't want to go back to the evil home she was a product of. In the new homeland, Ruth was noticed by a Godly man named Boaz and he pursued her and married her. Ruth became King David's great grandmother.

I now present Bathsheba to you. Bathsheba knows what you are going through if you've been lured into a relationship that destroyed your marriage. She was not a Jew. She was a Hittite. King David enticed Bathsheba into having a one-night stand. She didn't dare resist the flattery of the king. As may have happened to you, she became pregnant. David panicked. He tried to set up a situation where her husband would think the baby was his, but the plan didn't work. King David was too embarrassed to face the situation. He came up with a plan B and placed her husband on the front lines of the battle where he would surely be killed--and he was. But not all went well. The baby died. David fell into a deep depression. The bible doesn't speak of Bathsheba's mental state but I'm sure she suffered great despair. Later on, a man of God confronted King David about his sin. He repented. His depression was lifted. He began living for God again. Bathsheba became David's wife and gave birth to a child in Jesus' family tree.

The last woman deserves a special introduction. She is the mother of Jesus and her name is Mary. She is the only woman in Jesus' genealogy that is a Jew. She was engaged to marry a young man by the name of Joseph. Mary and Joseph chose to remain celibate and wait until the honeymoon night to consummate their love. But then the unthinkable thing happened. She became pregnant. Mary developed a bad reputation because she was an unwed mother. Do you know someone you have gossiped about who was in this situation? Her pregnancy was unique. She wasn't expecting a child as the result of a sin. The baby growing inside of her was conceived by the Holy Spirit. Don't think this scenario is so farfetched. Consider how God created life to begin with. Placing a God-life inside of Mary was no big deal for our big God. As the real-life story goes on, people judged Mary without knowing all the facts. That sort of thing happens to all of us at some time or other.

Life was hard for these women in Jesus' lifeline. But it was because of Jesus that they were loved, forgiven, recognized and recorded. They may have felt like their lives were useless and could easily have been thrown away like garbage. But Jesus recognized them as important in his life. They are important in our lives. They were included in the plan to bring Jesus into the world so he could save all of us.

Does your life resemble garbage? Parts of your life may feel torturous. Jesus knows your pain. He was tortured on the cross. He wants you to trade your life of torture in for his death of torture.

A Visit to the Counselor

You recognize that you are a tortured soul. It's time for a

torture trade-off intervention. You've scheduled an appointment to see the counselor. You already feel a little lighter just knowing that someone is going to help you. King David wants to add more hope to your day in Psalm 20:6 (MSG): "Help's coming, an answer's on the way, everything's going to work out." King David is advising you to expect healing and resolve.

The time of the appointment has arrived. You have signed in and have sat down in the waiting room. You now wait to be called back. You feel uptight, but hopeful. In a way, you want to back out and leave. It's hard to face hurtful feelings and memories. You're not sure if you can bear it. Satan's at it again. He wants you to be frightened off. He likes controlling you with fearful thoughts and emotions. He wants you to remain a scared little puppy. He knows if you reach healing you'll become a big cheerleader for God. He hates God.

While you are still contemplating leaving, the counselor calls you back. She greets you and says she's glad you're here. The counselor advises you that the success of this appointment depends on if you have the same goal in mind as she does. Her goal is for you to reach healing. She offers the option of leaving if all you want to do is numb the pain. You just want to survive. She wants you to thrive. It's at this time that she leads you into a moment of prayer to ask for God's special touch on the hour that you will be spending with her, to reveal the things that need to be dealt with, and to dissolve all fear and uncertainty. Amen.

She opens up the conversation by asking you some general questions about yourself. Then she asks the first critical question: "How may I help you?" She already knows that your life is a mess but she wants to hear your interpretation of it. You rattle off a list of people who have hurt you and caused your life to be a wreck. She nods her head and says "I see." She warns you to not be offended when she asks about the other side of the story regarding one or two your inflictors. She wants to teach you how to see the situation from a different angle, their angle. This technique will shed light on why you were hurt. It is meant to trade bitterness for empathy. It is her intention for you to use this method on the rest of the list of people you rattled off to her earlier.

Your counselor has chosen a set of questions that will lead you down a path to healing. It's important to answer honestly. Feel free to use emotion words. Messy lives are products of layers of hurt and pain. It helps to expose the pain and peel away the layers. It's a probability that you've never voiced how you feel aloud to anyone. It helps for someone to hear it and empathize with you. But remember that you want healing and resolve more than comfort and empathy. She gives you homework as you start out the door. Record your thoughts and feelings in a journal before going to sleep. Ask God to show you scripture that speaks to the situation. Don't be afraid to write down your problem areas. You can tear up the sheet of paper and throw it away. No one but God has to hear these words. Memorize and repeat the corrective verses to rewire your bad thinking system.

Your next visit arrives. She thinks you are ready to delve deeper. The counselor takes the questioning down an uncomfortable path. She asks: "Do you feel guilt and shame for the hurtful things done to you?" In other words, "Do you hold yourself responsible?" The counselor teaches you how to look at the situation from a different angle: "Did you ask for those things to be done to you?" The minute the words "no, I didn't" come out of your mouth is the minute you realize you have been feeling false guilt and shame. The guilty party is the one who forced the acts on you. God doesn't hold you accountable for that. She points out something important, though. Once you learn the truth, the way you live is totally on your account. You leave the office feeling a little lighter. Hope is on the horizon, but you're not at the horizon yet.

As the third week of counseling rolls around, you realize that facing scary facts isn't as scary as you thought. You begin to look forward to these visits. And then she asks, "Who allowed those people to hurt you?" You think about your answer but hesitate. This is the part that has scared you, scarred you, and slowly killed you. She encourages you to say it out loud. You finally blurt out, "It was God!" There, you said it! But now you feel awful for saying what you think is truth. You're afraid of being struck by lightning. But it seems once you say it the anger flows out like a river. You announce, "God stood by and watched those terrible things to be done to me, to be spoken to me, to mold me who I am today. It's his fault I have turned out this horrible way." You start sobbing uncontrollably. Your anger towards God leaves you feeling more guilty, confused, empty and disconnected from him. You think, "some Daddy he is."

She says, "I understand, but allow me to show you another side of the story." She shares that sin disconnects us from God. Sin breaks up relationships. When Adam sinned, he caused a rift between the whole human race and God. The people who hurt you are the ones who sinned. God doesn't sin. Which spirit do you think prompted the people who hurt you--God or Satan? God does not ask or want anyone to hurt anybody. God does not cause pain, Satan does. And yes, God is a good Daddy!! And now you can believe it!

Visit number four should be a good visit, right? It seems you have faced a lot of frightening things and you have survived and feel better than before. You even greet the counselor with a smile on your face. She asks you a curious question today. "What if you had grown up in a wonderful home with loving parents, fun vacations, and good school grades, made every team you tried out for, and had tons of friends?" "How would you have felt toward God?" And you answer, "God?" "That's right," she replies. The counselor explains that even though God doesn't tell anyone to hurt another person, he knows that such situations are the only way people may give him a second thought.

Think about how many of us Christians as children, grew up in Christian homes, attended church, enjoyed youth group functions, sang in the choir, but yet, don't allow God to influence our personal lives. We reserve God for Sundays only. God wants us to relate to him 24/7, 365. But instead, he gets once a week, maybe even only on Easter and Christmas. He expresses his desire for us in Ephesians 4:30 (MSG): "Don't grieve God. Don't break his heart. His Holy Spirit, moving and breathing in you, is the most intimate part of your life, making you fit for himself. Don't take such a gift for granted." How is your relationship with Daddy God? Is it broken? Is it thriving?

Your counselor knows that a tight relationship with God is the key to your healing. She wants to know if you want to continue on with the therapy and reach healing. You nod your head with a yes. You manage to whisper "show me how."

The disciples asked Jesus the same question. Listen to their conversation found in John 14:5b-6 (NLT): "So how can we know the way? Jesus told him, 'I am the way, the truth, and the life. No one can come to the Father except through me.'" I used this scripture earlier in this chapter to prove God wants to reconnect with us. But how is it that Jesus is the way? The answer is found in John 10:9 (NLT): "Yes, I am the gate. Those who come in through me will be saved. They will come and go freely and will find good pastures." We don't have gates leading into our yards here in America, but other parts of the world do. Gates are opportunities for protection. Jesus is asking you to walk up to his gate, talk to him face to face. He wants you to choose a lifetime of relationship with him. That choice also gets you a lifetime relationship with God and Holy Spirit.

You soak all of this information in. You tell your counselor "ok, I'm ready. What's the next step?" She tells you the same thing Jesus told his disciples in Matthew 14:24-25 (NLT): "Then Jesus said to his disciples, 'If any of you wants to be my follower, you must turn from your selfish ways, take up your cross, and follow me. If you try to hang onto your life, you will lose it. But if you give up your life for my sake, you will save it.'" She makes it easier to understand when she explains that "your cross" refers to "your torture." He wants you to trade your torture in for his.

Your counselor leans forward and looks you squarely in the eyes. You can sense the seriousness in her voice as she says, "You have to give up spending all your time comforting yourself. Comforting yourself is the same as feeling pity and becoming more depressed. The key to health and wholeness is to hang out with Jesus, get to know him, do what he says to do." She continues, "I know you're afraid of relationships. You avoid them because you always seem to get hurt." She suggests that moving forward in a relationship with Jesus is achieved by believing that he is for you and not against you. She points to John 10:10b where Jesus declares that he came to give you an abundant, thriving life, not a messy one. Then she asks you "Do you believe that Jesus really wants a relationship with you?" "Yes, I do," you reply. She sits up straight and smiles really big and declares the sentiment of Romans 6:22b (MSG): "A whole, healed, put-together life right now, with more and more of life on the way!"

The counselor suggests you do some more homework. You are instructed to go home and journal the names of those who have caused you pain. Ask Daddy God to help you forgive them of their actions. Verbally release them into God's care. Ask Father God to tell you what to do about the broken relationship. Thank him for his love and guidance. Then wait for him to give you instructions.

You walk out saying to God, "Ok, Father, help me with this relationship thing. I'm scared but I hope that I can have and enjoy relationships. Help me to get to know you better. Teach me how to love you the way you want me to love you because right now I don't know how to do that." Congratulate yourself; your real-life relationship with God has begun!

More Trees

Would it surprise you to find out that the Tree of Life in Genesis chapter 2 represents Jesus and The Tree of Knowledge of Good and Evil represents sin? Did you know that Jesus wants to make you into a good, strong, stately tree? That's what Isaiah 61: 3b (NCV) says: "They will be called Trees of Goodness, trees planted by the Lord to show his greatness."

Jesus tells a true but funny story about a blind man that he was healing. Jesus applied his spit to the man's eyes and put his hands on him. Then he asked the blind man if he could see anything. The blind man replies in Mark 8:24 (NIV): "He looked up and said, 'I see people, they look like trees walking around.'" Jesus then puts his hand on the man's eyes and his vision is restored. In a hazy glance, we look like trees.

So why all the references to trees? Trees start out from tiny seeds. The seeds die before being able to sprout to life. We, too, start out as life seeds, die to ourselves, and then sprout to new life through Jesus. Psalm 1:2-3 (MSG) tells how God's word can replant you as a tree: "Instead you thrill to God's Word. You chew on Scripture day and night. You're a tree replanted in Eden, bearing fresh fruit every month, never dropping a leaf, always in blossom."

Bad Trees

When you were visiting with the counselor, did you complain that your friends take advantage of you? Did you tell her that your dates are lousy people? I bet you were surprised when she told you that like-minded people are drawn to each other. Really, it makes sense. You are at home with people who are like you.

God agrees with your counselor. Notice the relationship qualities found in 2 Timothy 2:11-12 (NIRV): "Here is a saying you can trust. If we died with him, we will also live with him. If we don't give up, we will also rule with him. If we say we don't know him, he will also say he doesn't know us." In other words, if you are like-minded with Christ, he will guide you in his ways; cause his thoughts to be your thoughts, his quality of life to be your quality of life.

Good Tree

Today is the last session with your counselor. You're feeling a lot better than you were, but there's one more hurdle you can't seem to cross. Your past is haunting you. You share this information with her. She quickly informs you that sin is an identity theft. Sin (Satan) steals kills and destroys any good life you have, if you let it.

Identity theft takes place when we become so enmeshed in the effects of sin, the guilt and shame. It keeps us from growing as a person. Your counselor brings up an interesting fact. Sin, a wrongdoing, is a negative act that is ignited by negative emotion. A negative emotion can be changed by a Godly thought (or God's word). She says we humans give too much power to sin, power it really doesn't have. You ask her how sin affects relationships. She explains we tend to feel that God doesn't love us because of our past sins and we, then, don't love God because we think our sins have made us unlovable. Those same types of thoughts carry over to human love and relationships.

She points you to Romans 8:38-39 (Voice) for God's advice: "For I have every confidence that nothing--not death, life, heavenly messengers, dark spirits, the present, the future, spiritual powers, height, depth, nor any created thing--can come between us and the love of God revealed in the anointed, Jesus our Lord." She asks if you can see how sin is one of those things that cannot separate us from God's love once we have accepted salvation. You answer, "Yes." But you are plagued with a nagging thought. She sees the grimace on your face and asks you to voice your troubling thought. You tell her that it seems your love is tainted. She reminds you (and wants you to soak this in) that once you are rescued by Jesus, your sin life is nonexistent in his eyes.

The counselor asks you to look up Luke 10:27 (Voice) and read it out loud: "You shall love--love the Eternal One your God with everything you have: all your heart, all your soul, all your strength, and all your mind--and love your neighbor as yourself." She says,

"Daddy God doesn't consider you tainted, in fact, he wants your love badly. The counselor softly adds, "A mysterious thing happens when you love God with your beliefs, thoughts, emotions and actions. You soften up. You freely forgive others. You feel compassion. You start to view others as beautiful, worthy, lovable and full of potential." She goes on to tell you that you will want to reach out and connect and restore damaged relationships.

You walk out of her office for the last time determined to trust God with this love and relationship thing and let it grow into the beautiful experience he created it to be.

Daddy God's desire is for you to grow up into a healthy, good tree. We first discovered The Tree of Life in the Garden of Eden at the beginning of the bible in the book of Genesis. Now let me wow you with the fact that it pops up again at the end of the bible in God's home, heaven. Revelation 22:2 (NLT) describes the benefits of this wonderful tree: "On each side of the river grew a tree of life, bearing twelve crops of fruit, with a fresh crop each month. The leaves were used for medicine to heal the nations."

Daddy God and your counselor are so proud of you. So happy to be sharing life with you!

THE LOVE LIFE

Chapter Seven

You've heard my life story throughout the previous chapters. As a teenager, I sensed that the story of my life didn't add up with what a lot of other people were living before me. I remember going to the library while in Junior High School. I checked out books on etiquette thinking they would teach me a better way of living. The books of etiquette gave me rules to live by. Those rules satisfied me for a while.

I became adept at keeping the rules. The rules lead to a perfectionist lifestyle. I thought, "Surely no one could find fault with a perfect person." I also thought that perfect people were highly valued. What I didn't realize was that human perfectionism doesn't exist--except for one human, Jesus.

Jesus is the answer to a good life. He is the one who satisfies us. I boast that my middle-aged years are the best years of my life-- so far! I received healing by using the 21-Day Journal Notes system. That system straightened out a lot of misconceptions, including the perfectionism lifestyle. But still, I had a nagging feeling of being uncomfortable with myself. I felt unsettled about being me. It was like I was having a mental argument between myself and God's word. My life didn't match what God's word said it could be. And I didn't feel free to go to all lengths to develop my gifts and my worth. I felt stifled. It felt like a sin to grow myself--even for God's use.

How often do you hear someone claim "I love my life?" How

many times have you heard yourself say, "I hate my life??" I wanted to love the life I lived but I felt guilty about it.

The bible says that Jesus doesn't condemn us, yet I felt condemned. The bible says that Jesus died and rose again to new life so that I would not be guilty of sin, yet I felt guilty of all my sins. The bible says to not be afraid, to worry or be anxious, yet I was consumed with all three. The bible says we are to shine like stars and be his light, yet I felt dim and invisible.

I admit that I wanted to feel right and not condemned. I wanted to be free instead of being held back by guilt. I wanted to shine brightly for Jesus--not with a self-illuminating light, but as Jesus' light. I wanted to live in front of people the kind of life that would wow them and cause them to want Jesus in their lives.

Reasons Things Don't Add Up

There is a reason why a lot of us Christians are unsettled about who we are. Our thinking doesn't add up to what God's word says about us. We are afraid to live up to our God-potential for fear of becoming arrogant and proud. But what have we learned in this book about the origin of fear? Fear comes from Satan. Satan is using one sin to cause another sin. I call these soft sins, but still, the effect is to keep us down and low. One sin does not cancel out another. It sends us deeper down the wrong path. Satan doesn't want you to notice that I label our potential as God-potential, and not as self-potential. So arrogance and pride do not belong in this situation.

I think we Christians, under the lies of Satan, think humbleness means insignificance. God's intention is for us to be under his care, willing and wanting to please him, and then he raises us up to a new level of living.

The feelings of unworthiness block our reception of God's goodness and new life. We miss out on the experience of enjoying God and ourselves. It's possible that a fear of rejection from God keeps us from rising up. We've been rejected by people, so why wouldn't God reject us, too? Any time you feel fear just know that Satan is behind it. Rejection is a tool Satan loves to use, but it is just an emotion that can be changed by a God-thought.

Growing up in a depressed household (one or both parents depressed) teaches a child to stay down and low. If you grew up in this type of home, you may not realize that you were not taught to explore your gifts and talents as other children were taught. A depressed person doesn't want to be around people, go places, or do things. They live in a cocoon. The depressed person has no motivation. If this describes you, it's highly important for you to just follow God's word and do it even though you don't feel like doing it. A depressed person doesn't feel much of anything except sadness and doom.

A lot of people are afraid to let go and let God simply because they are afraid of God's plan for their lives. Did you notice the word "afraid" twice in the last sentence? Dear reader, God doesn't plan for everyone to be a preacher, missionary to Africa or to live in poverty. He does, however, have plans for people to be artists, teachers, nurses, lawyers, even good neighbors and shoppers. He needs Jesus-people all over the place. Whatever God has planned for you to do, you can be sure that you will enjoy it!

And one last reason that things don't add up is simply guilt. I felt too guilty to ask God for a good life because of my sins. It could be that you are unable (but really you are able) to let go of past sins, those you have committed, or those done to you. The good news is that Jesus has freed you from all of your sins. Romans 5:17 (TLB) says: "The sin of this one man, Adam, caused death to be king over all, but all who will take God's gift of forgiveness and acquittal are kings of life because of this one man, Jesus Christ." Consider that you haven't taken God's gift of forgiveness and acquittal. Father gave us Jesus so we can live the life of a king!

I think we may have some crazy thinking in our minds. When people get saved, they think of God as the New Sheriff in town. That's the type of relationship people had with God in the Old Testament times. I intend to challenge your way of thinking. After the Israelites refused to serve and love him, he handed out a set of laws, which we model our civil laws from. The relationship was a sheriff-type one where he measured our goodness by our willingness to obey those laws. Those laws were meant to show us that we couldn't be what the laws tell us to be. What God wanted us to admit to is, We Need God!

Before Adam and Eve sinned, they had a parent-child relationship with God. After Jesus died and rose to new life, he gave us the parent-child relationship back. I like to say we have a new Daddy in town, because he is unlike our earthly fathers. God no longer polices us. He now fathers us, grooms us and trains us. He loves and provides for us.

Love Me, Love Me Not

There's a lot of theological debate over the second half of Luke 10:27. It says we are to love our neighbor as ourselves. Some debaters say that it means it's ok to love ourselves. Others say that it means we already are sinful selfish beings and we naturally love ourselves. If the last statement is true, why would we, or God, want us to extend that type of love to others? In my opinion, neither of these explanations apply.

We forget that when we become followers of Jesus we stop being a "me" and become a "we." But note that Satan is quite happy with the church falling into the thought that God intends for us to love ourselves. The problem with loving ourselves is we tend to leave God out. If we don't need God's love then we don't need God for much of anything else. Romans 8:7 (MSG) opens our eyes to this unhealthy trend: "Anyone completely absorbed in self ignores God, ends up thinking more about self than God." It is the Holy Spirit living in us that makes us struggle with this type of self-love. We must remember that Father loves us first and then we love. Not the other way around.

Luke 10:27 starts with loving God with our total being-- thoughts, feelings, beliefs and actions. Next is to love neighbor and self. The key to loving self is to love God first. It ties in with giving up self. It is his love that energizes and motivates us to grow into wonderful people doing good things. Ephesians 3:20 (NIV) talks about what he can do with us: "Now to him who is able to do immeasurably more than all we ask or imagine according to His power that is at work within us." The lofty dreams you have inside of you can become reality because he lives in you.

Are you a negative-Nancy, feeling like God has no dreams or plans for your life? Think again! Or rather, think God-thoughts! 1 Corinthians 1:27-29 (MSG) says: "Isn't it obvious that God deliberately chose men and women that the culture overlooks and exploits and abuses, chose these 'nobodies' to expose the hollow pretentions of the 'somebodies'? That makes it quite clear that none of you can get by with blowing your own horn before God." Look at these verses this way: God living inside of us cancels out the self-hate and self-love.

You may be wondering how God expects us to love our neighbors if we don't love ourselves. And what about all those unlovable people around us? I'm sad to say we have ignored God; we haven't loved him as he wants us to. We've been trained to love people by the very people we are trying to love. But people don't love the way God loves.

Our thinking systems become weird when we try to love or please people. Did you know that a person can state an opinion to you, which may or may not have been intended to hurt you, yet you can spin it into weird thoughts that tear yourself down? It's true; I've done it so many times. But it's helpful to be aware that people may try some crazy things on you to get you to love them the way they think is appropriate.

Father warns us of our craziness in Jeremiah 17:9 (ESV): "The heart is deceitful above all things, and desperately sick; who can understand it?" He's telling us that our minds trick our own minds. That's why we have to retrain our minds using His word.

Father has a word of advice regarding pleasing people. It's found in Galatians 1:10 (Voice): "Do you think I care about the approval of men or about the approval of God? Do you think I am on a mission to please people? If I am still spinning my wheels trying to please men, then there is no way I can be a servant of the Anointed One, the Liberating King." He knows our initial response is to please people, but he's educating you to turn toward pleasing him. If you're pleasing him, you'll end up pleasing people, because he'll teach you how to relate to them and love them.

The Old Life Is Not Like the New Life

You know how you feel when you make up your mind to move from one home to another? You mentally shift attachment from one home to another. You pack up your belongings, make the journey to the new home and unpack. 2 Corinthians 5:17 (NLT) points out the decision to move from the old life to the new one: "Anyone who belongs to Christ has become a new person. The old life is gone, a new life has begun!"

It may be hard for you to grasp the concept of moving from the old life to the new one. Consider that living in the old life, the messed up one, is a representation of the "negative" you. The negative old life concentrates on the bad things that have happened to you or things you have done. The New life, is the new you. It is the same you, but a positive you. Your new life concentrates on the good things that have happened to you and good things you have done. It carries it forward and moves toward doing more good things.

Ephesians 4:22-23 (MSG) teaches us to clean out the old life (house): "Since, then we do not have the excuse of ignorance, everything--and I do mean everything--connected with that old way of life has to go. It's rotten through and through. Get rid of it! And then take on an entirely new way of life--a God-fashioned life." Verse 24 says: "a life renewed from the inside and working itself into your conduct as God accurately reproduces his character in you." Please, please, let God's word rewire your thinking system so you can live a God-fashioned life!

Praise God with Your Love

Being ok with yourself and loving yourself as God does is an act of praise to God. We can all agree that God deserves our best, but we tend to think we are at our best when we aren't sinning. Friend, God has already dealt with our sin. He wants you to think in a forward motion.

Jesus is the most well-known person of all history. He stands out to this very day. But why does he stand out? Why were the religious scholars amazed at the 12-year-old Jesus when he understood things of God and had the answers? Jesus is God and God knows everything there is to know. This same Jesus sent his Spirit, Holy Spirit, to live inside of us. Jesus wants us to stand out and represent him well. 1 Peter 2:12b (NCV) agrees with this: "Live such good lives that they will see the good things you do and will give glory to God on the day when Christ comes again."

Since being mentally healed, I've eagerly embraced change. I also love being different than others. I am not a cookie-cutter type person. I enjoy standing out in a good kind of way. I also like to help other people shine like stars (Philippians 2:15 b) by encouraging them, complimenting them, helping them to grow into their God-potential.

God created you into a beautiful being (Ephesians 2:10). Why wouldn't he want you to enjoy yourself? When you enjoy being yourself, you are offering up worship to him, because he lives in you. The truth is we humans have a weird habit of separating ourselves from God. We don't, or won't, mentally share in God's good pleasures, satisfactions and delights--even though we acknowledge that he lives in us.

Consider a few mental health advantages of sharing God's goodness in our lives.

1. Enjoying self dissolves defensiveness. I've had issues in the past with being defensive, but now that I enjoy my God-given self, I have no reason to be defensive.

2. Loving God with our total being colors everything we do with love and excitement.

3. You realize everyone can shine and live loud for God. The next time someone complains or whines you won't feel responsible for solving their problems. God is their solution. Share the good news with them.

4. Enjoying your life, growing and loving, helps you, the student, become the teacher--teaching others about Jesus and the new life he wants them to live.

5. No one can steal the real you--the you God made you to be. The fear and anger that results from injustice, melts away.

6. God's goodness helps us to not blow every situation out of proportion. He helps us to see the situation through his eyes.

7. Once we have our thinking system rewired with God's word, he protects us in another way. We are protected from the damaging comments made by others. When you really know the real you and like the real you, no one else's opinion matters.

8. It feels really good when you stop blaming others for your bad life----"what bad life?" It's mostly good, now!

God's Story of My Life

I have constructed a 21-Day Journal note that applies to each child of God. This note is longer than I normally put together--but it's an important one, one that tells the story of your new life. Pull out a notebook and handwrite this one out, once a day, times 21 days--or more if you need it. Enjoy the comfort and excitement as you think the truths God has given us. You can take it a step further and memorize it a paragraph at a time using the tips at the end of chapter three. Recite the paragraphs as you lay down at night or while taking a shower. Let God change you into a new person by changing the way you think about yourself.

Here it is--the story of your life as told by God:

Dear Father, I have been living a stunted and unsatisfying life.

My way of living is not working, so I'm exchanging it for your way. Thank you, Daddy God, for choosing me before I was conceived. I'm excited about the special work you have planned for my life (Jeremiah 1:5).

I am becoming a new person by exchanging my frenzied way of thinking for your calm and well-balanced way (Romans 12:2). I will do this by handwriting your words down and storing them in the recesses of my mind (Proverbs 7:3). Your word is healing me and rescuing me from the dark and scary places (Psalm 107:20).

I am comforted to know that you have forgiven me of all my sins (1 John 1:9). I am no longer holding onto guilt. I find it best to tell you about a wrongdoing as soon as I realize I've done a wrong (James 5:16). You are healing me. You are satisfying me with good things and making me feel young again (Psalm 103:3-5).

I recognize that fear and anger are from Satan (Ephesians 4:27). Thank you Lord, for gifting me with your power and love, calm and well-balanced mind, discipline and self-control (2 Timothy 1:7). I am moving away from pleasing people and moving toward pleasing you (Galatians 1:10).

It's refreshing to know you are filling me with new energy, power and desire (Philippians 2:13). I am now living my life to its fullest. I will live my God-potential life without guilt or hesitation (John 15:16). Thank you Father, for my new life! I love you and I live my new life for you! The end of journal note.

I no longer say "I love myself." I now say "I God-love myself." I no longer say "I hate my life." I now say "I love my God-given life." Now, I challenge you to worship God by loving the life God has given you!!

.

.

THE KINGDOM LIFE

Chapter Eight

A favorite memory of mine is that of the annual July 4th celebration at a former church. Family, friends, neighbors and the surrounding community would gather to the site on this day every year. Relaxation and excitement was built into the day. Good food was enjoyed, games were played and conversations were shared. Then, there was more to enjoy--the choir sang patriotic songs in grand fashion. But everyone knew the big show was soon going to happen--the big explosion in the sky. Fireworks galore. Eyes were gazing upward as folks sat on blankets and lawn chairs. The sight was spectacular!

I find myself looking up to the sky and past the clouds when I'm addressing Father God. He lives up there, you know. Any time I talk to him, I look up, that is, when I'm near a window. I like connecting with him in this way.

The 4th of July is a celebration of America separating from Mother England. Mother England was ruled by a king and the king passed laws regarding religion that our settlers didn't agree with. We became an independent country on July 4, 1776. The United States of America became self-reliant. We wrote up our own constitution, which was based on God's word.

The first English settlers came over to America and met the Indians who were already inhabitants of this great land. Two different kinds of people. Two different cultures. But soon there were people from other lands and cultures who joined the first two sets of people. The United States of America became a melting pot.

The melting pot has become a phenomenon in itself. America has become a people who are constantly struggling against each other. You find liberals proving conservatives wrong and vice versa. Atheists try to control the religious and the religious try to persuade atheists that there is the one true God. There are so many beliefs, cultures, systems, and ideas blended into one nation, so much so, that we seem to be confused and unsettled. The changing political theater makes us feel unstable and wobbly.

I wonder if being under the rule of one king might be an easier life. Some of you might debate against it saying a king could be mean and bad. I would counter your thought with the fact that our political leaders are mean and bad. Neither have our best interest in mind. Neither care about leading a nation under God's supervision.

I'm not claiming to be anti-American. On the contrary. America is the prime place to live out our God-potential lives. We are free to worship Him here and to serve him in many different ways. But the very freedom that brought us here has caused us problems. We are also free to ignore him. Many have lost sight of God, Jesus, and Holy Spirit.

Perhaps it would do us well to return to the kingdom lifestyle. We can do that even while living here in America. The perfect person to be crowned King is Jesus. Isaiah 11:1 (NCV) tells us that Jesus was born for this special role: "A new branch will grow from a stump of a tree; so a new king will come from the family of Jesse." We discovered in chapter six that the new king being referred to in this verse is not King David as one might think. The tree of life is a list of family members under a patriarchal name. Jesus is in the list under Jesse's name. Verse 2 (NCV) notes his qualities for this kingship: "The Spirit of the Lord will rest upon that King. The Spirit will give him wisdom and understanding, guidance and power. The Spirit will teach him to know and respect the Lord." Being born into royalty means that Jesus is intended to rule our lives for the entirety of his life. And since he is risen to new life, a life that never ends, that means we are to be ruled by him forever and ever. Once we become his servant and believe in him, we, too, have new life that goes on forever and ever. It's a perfect match!

The last paragraph starts out saying we would do well to return to the kingdom lifestyle. The fact is, we Christians are already there. Luke 17:21b (AMP) explains how this is possible: "The kingdom of God is within you [in your hearts]." Did you notice where the kingdom is located? It is in our hearts and minds, our souls. How big is Jesus' kingdom inside your mind?

1 Peter 2:9 (GWT) reveals our duty in Jesus' kingdom: "You are chosen people, a royal priesthood, a holy nation, people who belong to God. You were chosen to tell about the excellent qualities of God, who called you out of darkness into his marvelous light." Chances are you can't perform your priestly duty because you are still living the old life, in the darkness. Jesus is giving you an edict to move out of the darkness and into his kingdom of light and beauty, riches and provisions, health and restoration---the meaning of real freedom.

Consider the benefits of living under the rule of King Jesus. You don't have to be concerned about governmental things. God's government is governed by him. He has all the answers. He can arrange for anything to happen. All things are possible for him. And just by serving in his kingdom, you, too, have the reach of impossibilities as spoken in Mark 9:23b (GWT): "Everything is possible for the person who believes."

The king always selects the best of the best to do his work. You have been chosen to do his work as stated in 1 Peter 2:9 in a couple of paragraphs back. He's willing to make you the best of the best if you are willing to be the best of the best. Listen to his edict in Matthew 25:29 (TLB): "For the man who used well what he is given shall be given more and he shall have abundance. But the man who is unfaithful, even what little responsibility he has will be taken from him." Did you notice that the one who doesn't use his God-given talents and gifts to the best outcome is considered unfaithful?

I'm asking myself a couple of questions: what kind of people chooses not to be the best of the best? Why do people remain living the old life, in darkness, even though King Jesus lives in them? I think our individual minds are mixed up from the varying cultures and practices that have influenced our nation. We have believed the lies of Satan through influences from near and far and these beliefs have shaped us, left us in darkness. It would seem we have mingled too much with the ideas of the world and have incorporated them into our beliefs. For one moment pull your focus to Romans 6:16 (TLB): "Don't you realize that you can choose your own master? You can choose sin (with death) or else obedience (with acquittal). The one to whom you offer yourself-- he will take you and be your master, and you will be his slave." Does it sound like we are slaves, one way or another, period? I bring this up because some people probably revolt at the idea of being a slave, even to Jesus. But it seems that we are slaves no matter what we want or believe.

Suppose you choose not to be Christ's slave. Then who are you a slave to? Even if you say "no one is my master," you are in essence saying "I am my own master." 2 Peter 19b (GWT) says: "A person is a slave to whatever he gives in to." I'm afraid we've gone after the wrong type of freedom and have given in to ourselves. Allow me to show you ways we are slaves to ourselves.

We think we, alone, can control fear and anger in our lives. Yet, fear and anger end up controlling us.

We deny that jealousy and arrogance controls us. Yet, we can't resist the advantage and the significance we feel from these two enemies.

King Jesus wants to save you, avenge your hurt, give you his advantage. He wants to raise you up to his significance. He wants you to influence others with his authority in your life. You don't have to figure out how to forgive yourself; he's already taken care of it. And, raise your eyes, lift up your arms, let Jesus rescue you out of that dark pit.

This book reveals that Jesus has sent help for us servants. He gave Holy Spirit to us, to live inside of us. Holy Spirit gives us instructions, encourages us and heals us when we are wounded. God gave us his holy word. The Word gives us instructions, encourages us and heals us. God gave us Jesus, to show his love for us, to rescue us, to give us new life.

Take my life as an example. I used to be a slave to myself. I was a slave to fear, anger, jealousy, arrogance, control, guilt and depression. But I made a choice to be the best of the best for Jesus and his kingdom. My life has been healed, my skills sharpened, and now I am telling about God's excellent qualities who called me out of darkness and into his marvelous light.

I told you about the 21 Day Journal Notes that I developed back in chapter four. Now I want to share them with you, so you can be the best of the best for Jesus. I'm excited to reveal this prescriptive-type method. This method resolves the issue of not being able to control the thoughts. I am able to control my mental status much easier than before. My mind listens when I firmly tell myself "no" to a wrong thought. My Mind now recognizes the authority coming from my voice--it is God's authority in me.

The main prescription for this method is found in Proverbs 7:3 (TLB): "Write them down and also keep them deep within your heart." Here it is, God telling us to write down his words in a fashion that will soak it deep in our minds. The 21 Day Journal Notes produce the same results. I have separated them into categories for your convince and needs. Most are from my experiences that I feel are common to most people. Some were crafted for a friend's needs, but they, too, seemed common for lots of folks. A few are directed for people with life events that are different than mine. I think everything is covered, directly or indirectly. Read through them and mark the ones you need. You can work on one at a time or two or three. Handwrite the note once a day for 21 days. You'll feel a change in attitude by day 4 but continue on to day 21, or more if needed, for full healing. It's really easy to do. You'll feel peace and energy all at the same time while writing these out. My one request is that you include The Holy Relationships section whether you think you need them or not.

Holy Relationships

1. <u>Learn How to Love</u>: Luke 10:27 (TLB): "Love the Lord your God with all your heart, and with all you soul, and with all your strength, and with all your mind. And you must love your neighbor as yourself." Father, I don't know how to love nor do I know how to receive love. I am willing to love you but please help me, help me to love you the way you want me to. I am actively obeying your word as it leads me to the life you created me to enjoy. I am thriving in the love you have for me. Help me to love others the way you love them. Thank you for your devoted attention to me.

2. <u>Heavenly Authorities</u>: Ezekiel 36:26-27 (NCV): "I will teach

75

you to respect me completely and I will put a new way of thinking inside of you. I will take out the stubborn hearts of stone from your bodies, and I will give you obedient hearts of flesh. I will put my Spirit inside of you and help you to live by my rules and carefully obey my laws." Jesus, I haven't been serving you as king. I've been serving myself. I now recognize you as my King. I am following your advice, obeying you and guarding your words as my most precious possession. Thank you for being the best Master, ever. I love you Lord!

3. <u>Best Friends Forever</u>: John 14:26 (MSG): "The Friend, the Holy Spirit whom the Father will send at my request, will make everything plain to you. He will remind you of all the things I have told you. I'm leaving you well and whole." My dear Friend--Holy Spirit, you live inside of me. I am listening to you for guidance in my personal decisions and daily life routines. You are a beautiful gift from Jesus. Thank you for making me well and whole.

Fear

1. <u>Worried About Others Opinion of You</u>: Galatians 1:10 (NCV): Do you think I am trying to make people accept me? No, God is the One I am trying to please. Am I trying to please people? If I still wanted to please people, I would not be a servant of Christ." Jesus, I am moving away from pleasing others and moving toward pleasing you. Father, I am aligning myself with your plans and directions. Jesus, I am your servant. You are giving me a good life to enjoy. Thank you for freeing me from my worry of other's opinions.

2. <u>Stop Being Upset and Fearful</u>: John 14:27 (AMP): "Peace I leave with you; My [own] peace I now give and bequeath to you. Not as the world gives do I give to you. Do not let your hearts be troubled, neither let them be afraid. [Stop allowing yourselves to be agitated and disturbed; and do not permit yourselves to be fearful and intimidated and cowardly and unsettled.]" Jesus, I am accepting your loving gift of peace. Per your command, I will not allow myself to be agitated and disturbed. I will no longer permit myself to be fearful, intimidated, cowardly and unsettled. Your gift of peace is allowing me to live calmly, confidently and wholly--holy for you. Thank you for healing my fear!

3. <u>Fear of Rejection</u>: 2 Timothy 1:7 (AMP): "For God did not give us a spirit of timidity (of cowardice, of craven and cringing and

fawning fear), but [he has given us a Spirit] of power and love and of calm and well-balanced mind and discipline and self-control." My fear of future relational pain is from Satan. I refuse to feel this unnecessary fear. Father, I have your power and love infused in me. I have your sound mind to think rationally and calmly when in the middle of being relationally challenged. Holy Spirit, you are helping me to discipline myself so I can enjoy all of your wonderful gifts and promises. Future relational pain will sting but I will not be devastated.

4. <u>Anxiety, Panic Attacks</u>: Psalm 55:5 (GWT): "Fear and trembling have overcome me. Horror has overwhelmed me." Proverbs 29:25 (MSG): "The fear of human opinion disables; trusting in God protects you from that." Fear grips me. I admit that I allow it to control me. I will no longer trust this unnecessary fear. I will not permit myself to be disabled by others. My past is not my god. Dear Lord, I'm giving you the respect you alone deserve. I am spending time with you and getting to know you. Holy Spirit, heal my wounded heart so that I can grow and be used by you. Thank you Father for everything you are to me!

5. <u>Emotional Abandonment and Fear of Intimacy</u>: Psalm 27:10 (GWT): "Even if my father and mother abandon me, the Lord will take care of me." Psalm 34:18 (NLT): "The Lord is close to the brokenhearted; He rescues those who are crushed in spirit." 1 Corinthians 7:3 (NLT): "The husband should not deprive his wife of sexual intimacy, which is her right as a married woman, nor should the wife deprive her husband." Lord, I have a fear of intimacy. My childhood was dominated by depression, yelling and just being left alone. I recognize that my spirit was crushed. Lord, your hope wells up inside of me. I am your child, your family. You are my lifeline. I have your love, power, strength and courage infused in me to help me conquer this fear. From this day forward, I will seek to satisfy my husband/wife and he/she will satisfy me. Thank you for healing my spirit and energizing my marriage!

Anger

1. <u>Don't Keep Hurt Feelings Bottled up Inside</u>: Matthew 18:15-16 (MSG): "If a fellow believer hurts you, go and tell him-- work it out between the two of you. If he listens, you've made a friend. If he won't listen, take one or two others along so that the presence of witnesses will keep things honest, and try again."

When one of my friends hurt me, I will go to her/him and tell her/him how I feel. If she/he understands what I am feeling, then our friendship is stronger. If she/he doesn't understand, then I have the option to take another friend or two along so that the presence of others will help us all remain objective and hopefully salvage the relationship. If the situation remains unresolved then perhaps it's time to step away from the relationship.

2. Don't Beat Yourself Up: Romans 8:1 (GWT): "So those who are believers in Christ Jesus can no longer be condemned." I refuse to beat up myself and others for when we mess up. Jesus, you have already taken our beating. Thank you for the price you paid. Thank you that I am not charged for your wonderful act of love.

3. Haunted by The Ghost of Childhood Past: Proverbs 25:8 (MSG): "Don't jump to conclusions--there may be a perfectly good explanation for what you just saw." 1 John 4:18 (MSG): "There is no room in love for fear. Well-formed love banishes fear. Since fear is crippling, a fearful life--fear of death, fear of judgment--is one not yet fully formed in love." Lord, I admit to you that things done in my childhood birthed my fear. Fear has grown into anger as a shield of protection. I have dealt with my past in a wrong manner. I will research all sides of the story to gain an understanding of why the event happened. I want to feel empathy for the person who hurt me so that forgiveness can be real and applicable. With your help, I am not caving into fear or anger. I am bold because your boldness is inside of me. I am able to love because your love is in me. I am sensible and rational because I have your sound mind. Thank you Lord for your deepest love for me.

4. Verbal Explosion: Ephesians 4:31-32 (NLT): "Get rid of all bitterness, rage, anger, harsh words and slander, as well as all types of malicious behavior. Instead, be kind to each other, tenderhearted, forgiving one another, just as God through Christ has forgiven you." BOOM! I am being attacked verbally by an angry person. My usual response is for my thinking system to freeze and mentally run away. My past experience has been to interpret that the one who is projecting their anger on me was blaming me, rejecting me and not accepting my explanation. I misinterpreted their behavior as a sign that I was worthless. Lord, you have taught me that you live inside of me. I am infused with

your words, thoughts, wisdom as well as your forgiveness and compassion. I recognize that the angry person standing in front of me is full of problems and misery. His/her harsh words stem from a distorted thinking system. I am pausing and seeking you. You are helping me to remain calm and rational and I am speaking words of wisdom to this wounded person. Thank you Lord for planting your worth inside of me!

5. Church Family Business: Oh my goodness! It seems I have a personality clash with a church family member. We don't see eye to eye about a biblical teaching. I feel I'm right and my family member also feels right. Father, I know you see me as being right with you and you see my family member as being right with you. Open new understanding of your word to both of us. Reveal your truths and plant them in our minds. Thank you for loving on both of us.

Jealousy/Advantage

1. Tired of Being Mousy and Withdrawn: John 14:27 (MSG): "Peace. I don't leave you the way you're used to being left--feeling abandoned, bereft. Don't be upset. Don't be distraught." If only I could be like so-and-so. She stands tall and is confident. I recognize that I am mousy and withdrawn. It stems from being relationally challenged. They may taunt me, abandon me, reject me and even deprive me of a relationship, but Lord Jesus, you are always with me. I refuse to be intimidated, mousy and withdrawn. I am getting rid of doubt and mental conflict. These negatives, which show up as wimpy and scared, are very un-Jesus-like. Instead, I am standing tall, Jesus-confident. People are approaching me with a different attitude. I am enjoying displaying you, Jesus!

2. Overcome Jealousy: "Psalm 37:1, 7-9 (NIV): "Do not fret because of evil men or be envious of those who do wrong. Be still before the Lord and wait patiently for him; do not fret when men succeed in their ways, when they carry out their wicked schemes. Refrain from anger and turn from wrath; do not fret--it leads only to evil. For evil men will be cut off but those who hope in the Lord will inherit the land." Lord, I have been living a stagnant and unsatisfying life. Whenever I am around confident people my attitude quickly changes to an anxious mode. I don't know how to better myself. I become angry at the other person. He/she has

accomplished a better life. I recognize how my fretting and anxiousness has produced a bad behavior in me. I refuse to stay stuck in this angry rut toward people who don't deserve my anger. Father, I am now thriving in you and in your word. Thank you for my new and improved life!

3. <u>How Not to be Offended by Others</u>: 1 Corinthians 10:33 (GWT): "I don't think about what would be good for me but about what would be good for many people so that they might be saved." Proverbs 17:22 (NLT): "A cheerful heart is good medicine, but a broken spirit saps a person's strength." God, you have given me the ability to be sensitive to the emotions and body language of others. I have this ability to help them, and pray for them. I refuse to sabotage myself with this gift.

4. <u>Freedom!</u>: You, O Lord, are freedom! I confess that I am a slave to the enemy. It is mostly through my bad self-talk. I don't confer with you about decisions and thoughts. I admit that I throw my thoughts to the wind. Father, you are helping me to redirect my wind-tossed thoughts to you. Direct my daily living habits toward your desires and plans. I want to honor you and live freely. Galatians 5:16-17 (NLT): "So I advise you to live according to your new life in the Holy Spirit. Then you won't be doing what your sinful nature craves. The old sinful nature loves to do evil, which is just the opposite from what the Holy Spirit wants. And the Spirit gives us desires that are opposite from what the sinful nature desires. These two forces are constantly fighting each other, and your choices are never free from this conflict."

5. <u>Friendship Skills</u>: Father, I need to learn good friendship skills. I don't know how to do it or who to choose as a friend. You are the one who created relationships. Friendships are important according to John 15:13 (NIV): "Greater love has no one than this, that he lay down his life for his friends." Jesus, your examples of friendship building show me how to do it. The 12 men with 12 different personalities were chosen by you to represent you and to tell the good news about you. The story of your friendships with Mary, Martha and Lazarus is another good example. Jesus, I am learning and practicing your techniques. I will spend time and communicate with my new friends. Thank you for the generosity of your love.

6. <u>Yes, You are Beautiful!</u>: Ephesians 2:10 (NLT): "For we are God's masterpiece. He has created us anew in Christ Jesus, so we

can do the good things he planned for us long ago." Just imagine--I am a work of art! God, you say that I am beautiful and valuable! Why is this possible? Because you love me, Jesus! Father, you have good plans for me to accomplish. Jesus, your gifts and love are making it possible for me to clean up past negatives. The freedom and gratefulness bring me closer to you. I am using this beautiful life to serve you.

Arrogance

1. <u>Distrust</u>: Proverbs 3:5-6 (AMP): "Lean on, trust in, and be confident in the Lord with all your heart and mind and do not rely on your own insight or understanding. In all your ways know, recognize, and acknowledge Him and he will direct and make straight and plain your paths." Things have happened to me in the past that have caused me to be distrustful of anyone--even you, Lord. This has led me to commit a bad behavior, which is pride. I feel like I am the only one who can take care of me. Father, I am changing my bad feelings by exchanging my thoughts for your thoughts. When I find myself in a worrisome situation, I will rest in you and repeat over and over that I trust you. Thank you for filling me with your confidence!

2. <u>Unworthiness in the Eyes of my Authority</u>: Dear Dad, I want to be healed of unworthiness. My authority's actions remind me of past events that squelch my sense of worth. I defended my actions to my authority and was defeated. I realize my authority has his/her own significance and security issues. Father, you are helping me to break the cycle of messy feelings. Heal my old relational wounds and those of my authority. Thank you Lord for your truth and promises found in Deuteronomy 26:18b-19a (NIRV): "You are his special treasure. He promised that you would be. He has told you to keep all his commands. He has announced that he will make you famous. He'll give you more praise and honor than all the other nations he has made."

3. <u>Identity Tradeoff</u>: Jesus, you are my identity! My identity is not my addiction, compulsion, disability, or illness. I nurse my problem as if it's my baby. I have done it for so long that it feels like a part of me, like a baby, which is a lie of Satan. 2 Corinthians 5:21 (NLT): "For God made Christ, who never sinned, to be the offering for our sin, so that we could be made right with God through Christ." Jesus, you became my sin so I don't have to claim

81

it as my identity anymore. I am right with you, God. I am claiming this fact as I work through my problem. Thank you for making me whole.

Control

1. <u>Nix the Nag. Mix with Hubby/Wife</u>: Proverbs 21:23 (MSG): "Watch your words and hold your tongue; you'll save yourself a lot of grief." Yes, I am concerned about my husband's/wife's (problem), however, I will no longer bully him/her about it. I am freeing myself of this duty and turning it over to you, Lord. I trust you to talk to him/her about (problem). I will do good by focusing on his/her good traits and loving him/her. Being free from policing him/her will allow me to enjoy our relationship better. Lord, thank you for honoring my request to help me and my spouse.

2. <u>Busyness</u>: Psalm 127:2 (MSG): "It's useless to rise early and go to bed late, and work your worried fingers to the bone. Don't you know he enjoys giving rest to those he loves?" Proverbs 14:30 (AMP): "A calm and undisturbed mind and heart are the life and health of the body, but envy, jealousy, and wrath are like rottenness of the bones." Who has control over busyness? I do! But why do I feel it necessary to always be on the go? I have a new life in you, Jesus. I am free from my prison of "never having enough time." I am refusing to belittle myself because I do not have the things my neighbors have. I will no longer treat my body and mind as though I want to kill myself. I am living at your pace. I am feeling your calmness and rest.

3. <u>Blockage</u>: 1 Corinthians 10:19-22 (MSG): "Do you see the difference? Sacrifice offered to idols are offered to nothing, for what's the idol but a nothing? Or worse than nothing, a minus, a demon! I don't want you to become part of something that reduces you to less than yourself. And you can't have it both ways, banqueting with the Master one day and slumming with the demons the next. Besides, the Master won't put up with it. He wants us--all or nothing. Do you think you can get off with anything less?" My eyes and mind have not been on you, Lord. I have allowed outside influences to control me. I find myself encouraging and nursing my sins. I am sinning and sin is blocking you out of my mind. You give me confidence to face my challenges. I am comforted that you are holding my hand through

this process. You won't let me fail. Praise you!

4. Who's in Control?: Philippians 4:6-7 (MSG): "Don't fret or worry. Instead of worrying, pray. Let petitions and praises shape your worries into prayers, letting God know your concerns. Before you know it, a sense of God's wholeness, everything coming together for good, will come and settle you down. It's wonderful what happens when Christ displaces worry at the center of your life." I get so stressed out when I am dealing with a difficult person. I feel loss of respect. I spiral out of control trying to gain control of my situation. I am to look at myself as the problem and not the other person. There will always be people in my life that I will never be able to control. However, I have control over me with your help. Lord, I give these difficult times to you and trust you to keep me grounded. Thank you, Lord!

5. Family Busyness: Father, I have placed all of my children and grandchildren into your care. Love them, use them, help them to love you and serve you. You are giving good, God-health and wholeness to my family. You are straightening out the wrongs that I modeled to them. Thank you that you have made them right with you. Ephesians 5:1-2 (MSG): "Watch what God does and then you do it, like children who learn proper behavior from their parents. Mostly what God does is love you. Keep company with him and learn a life of love. Observe how Christ loved us. His love was not cautious but extravagant. He didn't love in order to get something from us but to give everything of himself to us. Love like that."

Guilt

1. Really Bad Decisions: Lord Jesus, I am painfully admitting to you that in the past I have committed really bad sins. Lord, I know that addictions, abortion, sexual promiscuity, fantasies, cheating, lying, gossiping, stealing, abusing others, abandonment, bullying are all terribly wrong. The things I am guilty of are weighing heavily on my mind and have been for a long time. It consumes me and controls me. I am ready to give it up and give it to you. I am reading Psalm 32:1 (NLT) that advises me: "Oh, what joy for those whose rebellion is forgiven, whose sin is put out of sight!" Father, help me to accept your forgiveness and love. I read in Matthew 12:32 (MSG): "If you reject the Son of Man out of some misunderstanding, the Holy Spirit can forgive you, but

when you reject the Holy Spirit, you're sawing off the branch on which you're sitting, severing by your own perversity all connection with the One who forgives." Holy Spirit, I accept you, I am forgiven. I am ok! Lord, help me to forgive others who may have contributed to the state I found myself in at the time of my sins. Lord, heal my heart from this grief. Thank you immensely!

2. Thanks for Straightening Me Out: No one, except you, have straightened me out. My motives, desires and actions have all changed in response to my love for you. I can see why your number one command is to love you with our total beings. It has softened me. It has energized me. I must now admit that it is not my responsibility to straighten out every Christian whom I don't agree with. That is your job, Father, unless you give me guidance to do it--then I will do it with a tone of love. 1 Peter 3:10-11 (AMP): "For let him who wants to enjoy life and see good days [good-whether apparent or not] keep his tongue free from evil and his lips from guile (treachery, deceit). Let him turn away from wickedness and shun it, and let him do right. Let him search for peace (harmony; freedom from fears, agitating passions, and moral conflicts) and seek it eagerly. [Do not merely desire peaceful relations with God, with your fellowmen, and with yourself, but pursue, go after them!]"

3. Human Craziness: Father, I am swamped with feelings and thoughts of condemnation, guilt and put-downs over the silliest and craziest things. The real truth is found in 1 John 3:21-22 (MSG): "And friends, once that's taken care of and we're no longer accusing or condemning ourselves, we're bold and free before God! We're able to stretch our hands out and receive what we asked for because we're pleasing him." I have been sabotaging myself. Father, help me to consciously and deliberately refuse to condemn myself and others. Thank you Jesus, that you gave your life to pay for my sins. Thank you Father, for raising Jesus from the dead to give me new life and freedom! Highest praises to you!

Depression

1. Invisible: Ephesians 4:21-24 (MSG): "That's no life for you. You learned Christ! We do not have the excuse of ignorance, everything--and I do mean everything--connected with that old way of life has to go. It's rotten through and through. Get rid of it! And then take on an entirely new way of life--a God-fashioned life,

a life renewed from the inside and working itself into your conduct as God accurately reproduces His character in you." I feel invisible. I feel no passion. No interest. No energy. No creativity. I am floating along in life with no purpose or direction. I feel lost in the crowd. Because of your word, I realize I am on a dead-end path. This dead-end path is not your path. I chose this day to be led and directed by you. Help me to love you, Lord, with my whole being. Help me to share your characteristics, your loves, your ways. I refuse to live lifeless. My goal is to be renewed and refreshed. I want to add color and flavor to my life so that you will be visible in me. You are such an amazing God!

2. Sick and Tired: I am sick and tired of my life. My life is a mess and is causing me to be physically sick and fatigued all the time. Jesus, you are asking me in Matthew 11:28-30 (MSG): "Are you tired? Worn out? Burned out on religion? Come to me. Get away with me. And you'll recover your life. I'll show you how to take a real rest. Walk with me and work with me--watch how I do it. Learn the unforced rhythms of grace. I won't lay anything heavy or ill-fitting on you. Keep company with me and you'll learn to live freely and lightly." As I recognize fatigue and illness, I will ask you, Father, to reveal the source of my infliction. Then I will follow the plan you have laid out for me in your word. Life flowing forward is wonderful! Light and free living is beautiful! Thank you Jesus!

3. Sad, So Sad!: Psalm 42:11 (Voice): "Why am I so overwrought, why am I so disturbed? Why can't I just hope in God? Despite all my emotions, I will believe and praise the One who saves me, my God." Psalm 103:5 (Voice): "When your soul is famished and withering, He fills you with good and beautiful things, satisfying you as long as you live. He makes you strong like an eagle, restoring your youth." I am overcome with despair and sadness. Hope doesn't seem to be an option. My life is full of gloom and doom. My appetite and sleep are affected. I can't think straight. I don't have the energy to rise up and beat this thing. I'm surprised to find your words of hope and healing for me. I am refusing to let my emotions rule my life. I am believing you and praising you. You are lifting this gloom and doom. You are replacing it with beautiful and satisfying things. Thank you for making me young again!

Mental Abuse

1. <u>Rejection</u>: I am suffering from double rejection. I am angry with my mother/father who has tried to kill my soul. I am deeply hurt by my mom/dad who chooses to let herself/himself be controlled by my father/mother and be separated from me. Holy Father, you tell me in Psalm 27:10 (NIV): "Though my father and mother forsake me, the Lord will receive me." Thank you for making me your dearly loved daughter. I am receiving my new life from your word according to 1 Peter 1:23 (MSG): "Your new life is not like your old life. Your old birth came from mortal sperm; your new birth comes from God's living word."

2. <u>Mental abuse</u>: I am suffering from mental abuse. I recognize that my mother/father molded me into a dysfunctional mess. I no longer try to reason with her/him. Jesus, I am trading in my torture for your torture on the cross. Jesus, you are rescuing me as stated in Psalm 107:20 (AMP): "He sends forth his word and heals them and rescues them from the pit and destruction." I am turning to your word for good mental health as promised in Proverbs 4:21-23 (NCV): "Don't ever forget my words; keep them always in mind. They are the key to life for those who find them; they bring health to the whole body. Be careful what you think, because your thoughts run your life." Jesus, I am thinking your words in my mind instead of my mother's/father's words. Thank you for giving me good mental health!

3. <u>Love and Feelings</u>: I suffer pain from childhood wounds caused by my mother's/father's inability to love me. I also suffer from people stealing my right to own my feelings. Father, I cherish that you chose me before my mother/father had a chance to as stated in Jeremiah 1:5 (NCV): "Before I made you in your mother's womb, I chose you. Before you were born, I set you apart for a special work." I am learning to believe and receive all of your goodness as taught in 1 John 3:21-22 (MSG): "And friends, once that's taken care of and we're no longer accusing or condemning ourselves, we're bold and free before God! We're able to stretch our hands out and receive what we asked for because we're doing what pleases him." Thank you Father, for healing my wounds and memories. Thank you for showing me the right way to live.

Encouragement

1. Safe While I'm Serving: Father, I've committed to serve you, however, I am being overtaken by negative energy of the ones I am ministering to. Help me to help them. Remind me of Psalm 91:2 (NCV): "I will say to the Lord, 'You are my place of safety and protection. You are my God and I trust you.'" Lord, thank you for the changes that I can see and the ones I don't see. I am surrendering to you the ones I am ministering to. I am waiting and listening for your orders. Thank you for the opposition as it means Satan doesn't like what you are accomplishing. Psalm 92:13-14 (NCV): "Like trees planted in the Temple of the Lord, they will grow strong in the courtyards of our God. When they are old, they will still produce fruit; they will be healthy and fresh."

2. What am I Supposed to do?: Dear Father, you have healed me in so many areas of wrongful beliefs. Because of your healing, a whole new world of opportunities has opened up to me. With the cloudiness of negative thinking out of the way, I can now identify the gifts you have given me. Please give me clear, concise directions so that I can serve you the way you want me to. Your word says that you have special plans for me and a wonderful life. I know it to be true. Thank you so much! Philippians 1:6 (Voice): "I am confident that the Creator, who has begun such a great work among you, will not stop in mid-design but will keep perfecting you until the day Jesus, the Anointed, our Liberating King, returns to redeem the world."

3. I am OK!: Thank you Father--You have made me ok! There are times when I feel wobbly and unsure of myself, but there you are, steadying me and helping me to stand straight and tall. Father, you are my lover. Holy Spirit, you are my consoler. Jesus, you are my supernatural mentor. Romans 8:28 (AMP) assures me that I am ok: "We are assured and know that [God being a partner in their labor] all things work together and are [fitting into a plan] for good to and for those who love God and are called according to [His] design and purpose." Thank you for showing me your purpose and design for my life. I am yours--take me and use me and grow me. I love you!

Dear Reader, I hope you enjoy the process of transformation as much as I did. The supernatural effects I felt were: restfulness, yet energetic. Releasing myself to God, only to be elevated to a new level. Willing to give up my types of fun and fulfillment, but experiencing explosion of his pleasure and delight. My frustration melted away and replaced by satisfaction.

Father wants to unveil your future. Take on the new life because it is yours! Do what 1 Peter 1:13-16 MSG) says: "So roll up your sleeves, put your mind in gear, be totally ready to receive the gift that's coming when Jesus arrives. Don't lazily slip back into those old grooves of evil, doing what you feel like doing. You didn't know any better then; you do now. As obedient children, let yourselves be pulled into a way of life shaped by God's life, a life energetic and blazing with holiness. God said, 'I am holy; you be holy.'"

You've been given a prescription of God's good health. Take it compliantly. Be rehabbed and renewed and refreshed. He has work for you to do!

THE LISTENING LIFE

Chapter Nine

A voiceless person craves to be heard, I know because I was voiceless in my old life. A voiceless person is not heard because they don't feel like they have anything of worth to be said. The lack of worth that a voiceless person feels affects everything about him/herself including the voice. It's really the mind that is affected. Words are a product of thoughts and thoughts are a product of worth.

The word "worth" is a moving-type word. It means to be "good" and also to "become." You should feel a little bit lifted up in spirits if you are a voiceless person. Your worth status can change! Isn't that wonderful? As a Christian, you are already "good" in God's eyes. I just have to convince you to accept God's good, and then you'll keep moving forward doing good and feeling good. Good is a forward moving spirit. To become anything requires moving toward the thing. You just have to start moving. Moving forward starts with listening--to God.

What are Signs of Not Listening?

You, my friend, are not totally voiceless. You carry on conversations every day. If you speak timidly, then your words will be received timidly. If you speak in an agitated manner then the other person will respond in a defensive way. If you interrupt the other person during a conversation the other person will shut down. If you feel distracted while listening to someone then the other person will soon stop and walk away. If you answer with limited amount of words (yes or no, instead of yes and why) then the conversation will be very short. Your peers probably consider you a boring person with no personality. But I'm not going to let you be the boring, no-personality person for long. You're going to learn how to listen and how to be listened to.

Why is Listening Such a Hard Thing to do?

Listening is a skill that requires a person to focus, to consider, and understand the one you are listening to. You have to, let me repeat, you have to take in the other person's words, weigh them in your mind, consider their circumstance and display a sense of understanding. Self-discipline (which is a gift or help from the Holy Spirit) is an essential ingredient to the art of listening. A clear mind is a must to successfully engage with another person.

Hyper-mindedness is the culprit for listening failure. James 1:8 (NCV) describes this mental problem in detail: "Such doubters are thinking two different things at the same time, and they cannot decide about anything they do. They should not think they would receive anything from the Lord." The battle going on in the doubter's mind is between God and Satan. God wants you to accept that he sees you as good. Satan convinces you that you're not good. You are constantly debating the two scenarios during every conversation you have. You really aren't consciously present when talking to another person. Satan has you mentally unstable and confused. No wonder people run away from you.

I Want to Learn How to Listen

1 Peter 5:8 (GWT) explains the importance of mental health: "Keep your mind clear, and be alert. Your opponent the devil is prowling around like a roaring lion as he looks for someone to devour." You see, the 21 Day Journal Notes heal the mental attacks from Satan. Hyper-mindedness is caused when Satan attacks our minds. Hyper-mindedness is caused by fear/anxiety, anger, jealousy, arrogance, control, guilt and depression.

Once you have entered your new mental life you can hear and be heard much easier. God wants you to come to him in your mind as per Psalm 46:10 (Voice): "Be still, be calm, see, and understand I am the True God. I am honored among all the nations. I am honored over all the earth." God didn't start listening to me until I started listening to him. Listening is a form of honor and respect.

Key words found in the bible that equal to "listening" are "draw near" and "seek." Listen to the attention paid to the state of the mind in James 4:8 (Voice): "Come close to the one true God, and He will draw close to you...Cleanse your heart, because your mind is split down the middle, your love for God on one side and selfish pursuits on the other." You can hear references to the battle in your mind between God and Satan, or in this case, yourself. God is no different than your peers; he just walks away from this type of conversation.

Jeremiah 29:12-13 (TLB) tells the conditions of a conversation he'll stick around for: "In those days when you pray, I will listen. You will find me when you seek me, if you look for me in earnest." This verse is important to listening because it symbolizes a declaration on your part to be loyal to God. That's when he will listen to you. You'll feel a calm and comfort when you realize he's answered your prayer. If you have any question as to if it's God or Satan or yourself answering a prayer, just take the feel test of your emotions. Do you feel agitated or do you feel peacefulness? Negativity and bad thoughts come from Satan and yourself. Positivity and goodness come from God. Agitation is implanted by evil and peacefulness is a gift of Holy Spirit. If you have doubt about an answer remember that doubt comes from Satan and faith comes from God.

What are the Benefits of Listening?

The art of conversation consists of talking and listening. You share ideas and thoughts through talking. You receive knowledge of the other person through listening.

Relationships can be repaired as two people truly listen to each other. It's smart to pick up on key words from the other person. Ask a question for clarity regarding a key word. Resolve happens when one understands the other side of the story.

Listening is a tool for learning from a teacher, a minister, even a helpful coworker or neighbor. Advise is meant to help you live a better life. God wants you to enjoy the life he has given you.

Wake Up and Listen

God gets really tired of us not listening to him just as we get frustrated for the same treatment. We feel loss of respect and worth--so does he. We don't feel understood, yet, he does understand, but feels slighted because we won't tell him about our problems. When we do cry to him during a crisis, we don't stick around long to honor him and love him for what he has helped us with.

One of the ways we don't listen to him is by ignoring his word. You may puff up and declare that you do read his word. But I'll challenge your listening skills by asking you why you don't believe what he says about you, about the things you are going through, about anything.

Listen to God as he tells you how your treatment of him comes back to haunt you in Obadiah 1:15b (MSG): "As you have done, it will be done to you. What you did will boomerang back and hit your own head." And Jesus echoes the same sentiment in Matthew 7:2 (TLB): "For others will treat you as you treat them." These two pieces of advice don't just apply to human relationships.

I've been working on this book for two years now. A few months ago, I wondered why it was taking me so long. I had such a hard time getting my mind to focus and write the good things I knew God wanted me to. So I asked God about it. He referred me to Matthew 7:2--that's when I knew this verse applied to Him, too. I listened to God and made a new commitment to him. I started keeping regular writing hours. Before that commitment, I would get started late in the day and nap when I felt like it. I knew he had listened to me when I noticed a sharp difference in my writing efforts. Tons of ideas flowed in my mind and onto paper. Want to hear something crazy? I felt like a professional writer even as I sat in my living room in sweat pants. All of this happened the next day following my conversation with him. My confidence level rose to new heights because I listened to God.

You may be wondering how you can hear from God? I know I sound like a broken record, but praying and reading the bible is the answer. Your attitude is also a key element--do it because you are serious about connecting with him--he can detect seriousness in a heartbeat.

Consider how many verses are repeated over and over in the bible. Luke 10:27 is one of the many verses that pull us to him. It is an important verse as it is the new first and second commandments following the new life era. Luke 10:27 (Voice) clearly says: "You shall love---'love the Eternal One your God with everything you have: all your heart, all your soul, all your strength, and all your mind'--and 'love your neighbors as yourself.'" Father didn't write it down several times for you to disobey it or disbelieve it. He doesn't like to be ignored any more than you do.

It's a well-known fact that there are 365 verses in the bible telling us not to be afraid and fearful. What does it take for us to listen?

I can say that I truly love God. He healed me with his word and I am very grateful. But I had a notion in my mind one day to ask him to help me love him the way he wanted me to. I thought, "Ok, I'll ask him." Wow! He listened to my request. I thought I loved him before, but now I love him deeply. It turned out to be one of the biggest gifts he has given me. It has changed my response to everything. Loving him the way he wants me to (with his help) has softened me. I am able to forgive much easier and quicker. I feel more compassion. I feel a love for others that I didn't have before. I find I'm not defensive when someone throws a zinger my way. I just wish you could experience the same gift.

Need Good Reception?

My heart was hardened and I didn't realize it until God softened it. Our heart is the mind, soul, the communication center between us and God. Things, even ourselves, can block information going either way.

Keevin and I have lived in mountainous areas. You know the situation of cell reception if you've ever vacationed in one of the mountains. Our cell reception could be strong or it could be spotty. It depended on the location we were in and if a mountain was blocking the tower. Service could be restored when we turned a curve or traveled down the mountain. Our communication with God is similar. Sin and bad behavior (caused from bad emotions) become the mountains that block off reception. God wants us to know he hasn't moved. I love how Proverbs 18:10 (AMP) proves he is our tower: "The name of the Lord is a strong tower; the [consistently] righteous man [upright and in right standing with God] runs into it and is safe, high [above evil] and strong." Did you hear God telling us to run toward him? He's still where he is. We are the ones who need to move.

We laugh when a TV show portrays someone going to great lengths to find a little bit of coveted signal. How often do we search for God and reach out to him? At what lengths are you willing to reach him? You could do like I did and get up at 4:45 a.m. to spend 15 minutes with him in prayer and bible reading. That little bit of time and effort has grown to an all-day contact with Father. I talk to him all the time. I talk to him out loud. I sing to him. I talk to him in my thoughts. I love him with my mind and actions. It is a 24/7, 365 relationship that started from 15 minutes a day at 4:45 a.m.

So how do you move away from the blocked signal known as sin? The only way to move toward God is to move away from blockage in your mind. Start out by listening to him instead of your sin/bad emotions. Catch the mind-pointing words found in Matthew 13:9 (AMP): "He who has ears [to hear], let him be listening and let him consider and perceive and comprehend by hearing." The three words, consider, perceive and comprehend, all point to the mind. That mind of yours is an important place of reception on your side of the conversation.

Fantasies, escapisms (books, TV, games), and nursing our wounds are ways we try to do over or undo what was done to us, usually in childhood. Even picking the wrong mate over and over is an attempt to please someone from the past. God says the way to do over or undo those events is to confront those events head on in your mind using God's word. James 1:2 (Voice) is one of the many verses telling us to face our trials and hardships (code word for sin and bad emotions or situations beyond our control): "Don't run from tests and hardships, brothers and sisters. As difficult as they are, you will ultimately find joy in them;" Imagine the relief and feeling of accomplishment when you realize you (with God) are bigger and stronger than that sin, bad emotion and out of control situation. Verse 3 (Voice) explains the process: "If you embrace them, your faith will blossom under pressure and teach you true patience as you endure." And the process continues exposing good results in verse 4: "And true patience brought on by endurance will equip you to complete the journey and cross the finish line-- mature, complete, and wanting nothing." Now, doesn't that sound like a great do over or undoing? But grasp what verse 5 says: "If you don't have all the wisdom needed for this journey, then all you have to do is ask God for it; and God will grant all that you need.

He gives lavishly and never scolds you for asking." Dear reader, you have no excuse to remain unhealthy!

There Really is a Better Way

Listening to God's direction uncomplicated life. The energies used for making decisions are freed up so you can do other things well. Stress is reduced by living under God's good plan. Matthew 13:12 (NLT) explains the pros and cons of listening to God: "To those who are open to my teaching, more understanding will be given, and they will have an abundance of knowledge. But to those who are not listening, even what they have will be taken away from them."

I want to ask you a curious question. After reading about God's good plans for your life, and the way he can help you out of your bad situations, have you decided to commit to him? Or are you still wavering as to whether to commit or not? If the latter is true for you, consider that you don't know the true state of your being. You don't have all the facts needed to make that decision! Isaiah 28:15b (GWT) exposes a truth we don't like to admit to: "We have taken refuge in our lies, and falsehood is our hiding place." Why do we lie to ourselves? It seems as if we are a traitor to ourselves. But really, it is God whom we are betraying. Our self is happy to hide behind falsehoods in order to remain independent.

I'm afraid we've believed Satan's lies about our independence. Matthew 13:15 (NCV) alludes to our misfortune: "For the minds of these people have become stubborn. They do not hear with their ears, and they have closed their eyes. Otherwise, they might really understand what they see with their eyes and hear with their ears. They might really understand in their minds and come back to me and be healed." You're allowing your mind and thoughts to be stubborn. Your stubbornness is costing you good health.

It's a high probability that you grew up undernourished, under loved, under accepted and undervalued. You're used to being all under. I get it. God gets it---but he wants you to rise up from down under and come up to his level. Pray Psalm 119:8 (NCV) to Father: "Open my eyes to see the miracles in your teaching."

You've been taught so many bad ways that it feels biblical to you. Mark 7:13 (NIV) encourages you to look at your former teachings and compare them to God's teachings: "Thus you nullify the word of God by your tradition that you have handed down. And you do many things like that." It's time to listen, really listen to God's word.

Do You Trust Him Enough to Listen to Him?

Are you able to relax and have fun? How's your mental health? Mental health and spiritual health impact each other. Listening to God's spiritual words improves our health. Proverbs 4:20-22 (MSG) proves the health theory: "Dear friend, listen well to my words; tune your ears to my voice. Keep my message in plain view at all times. Concentrate! Learn it by heart! Those who discover these words live really live; body and soul, they're bursting with health." Do I need to bring up the benefits of bible memorization? What if you find yourself at a low point right now? It's understandable since you've been living down under. Father is so kind to us that he makes up the difference in where we are. 2 Corinthians 12:9 (GWT) comforts and energizes us: "But he told me: 'My kindness is all you need. My power is strongest when you are weak.'" You are not too far under to be unreachable. In fact, it's his plan to show you what he can do for you when you are too weak, too low, to help yourself.

So many of us have made the mistake of receiving salvation but not living out the salvation. Just picture yourself in a jail cell that Jesus has unlocked and opened up. He's standing on the outside wondering why you're not willing to come out to him. Philippians 3:14 (MSG) reveals the upper level life that is waiting for you, courtesy of Jesus: "I press on toward the goal for the prize of the upward call of God in Christ Jesus." Listen to the apostle Paul. Listen to Jesus. Listen to God. Listen to Holy Spirit--after all, you are one with him.

Come on out! Enjoy your new salvation life!

THE BEAUTIFUL LIFE

Chapter Ten

In the early days of my ministry, I had a craving of sorts to reach out to women, to lift up their spirits. I knew that all women are obsessed with beauty, so I chose beauty as a means to reach them. I designed a card with the words "All Women Are Beautiful" on one side and on the other side, I typed Ephesians 2:10 (NLT): "For we are God's masterpiece. He has created us anew in Christ Jesus, so that we can do the good things He planned for us long ago."

Why do we want to look beautiful? Because we know that beauty attracts people! We think the only way to be loved, accepted and viewed as worthy is to be beautiful. We start and grow relationships based on the level of attractiveness our minds deem worthy. We use beauty like a book cover. The problem is the story inside the book doesn't match the cover.

Satan has distorted our desire to be beautiful. We have bought into his lie that being beautiful is the only way to have relationships, to be loved. The concept of beauty is mislabeled from magazine articles to infomercials. These ideas are superficial and unnatural. They don't generate a lasting effect. We have adopted a pattern of thinking that the flaws of our bodies make us totally undesirable. Can you explain why a woman still sees herself as fat after she has lost a lot of weight? Think about your answer and see if it matches my suspicions. I'll revisit the question later in this chapter.

The Story of a Beautiful Lady

I want to share a story that I found in the bible about a beautiful lady. See if it sounds a lot like yourself. We'll stop at intervals and discuss it. The story begins in Ezekiel 16:1-5 (GWT): "The Lord spoke his word to me. He said 'Son of man, make known to the people of Jerusalem the disgusting things they have done. Tell them, this is what the Almighty Lord says to the people of Jerusalem: Your birthplace and your ancestors were in the land of the Canaanites. Your father was an Amorite, and your mother was a Hittite. When you were born, your umbilical cord wasn't cut. You weren't washed with water to make you clean. You weren't rubbed with salt or wrapped in cloth. No one who saw you felt sorry enough for you to do any of these things. But you were thrown into an open field. You were rejected when you were born.'" The background information for this story transports us back to ancient times. The Israelites came from a pagan background and worshipped dead idols. The ancestors conjured up ideas that the idols were telling them to dispose of their baby girls. Do you feel rejected and thrown away like these baby girls? The Lord is using the story as an analogy of Israel being the unfaithful wife and God being the faithful husband.

And the story continues, Ezekiel 16:8 (GWT): "I went by you again and looked at you. You were old enough to make love to. So I spread my robe over you and covered your naked body. I promised to love you, and I exchanged marriage vows with you. You became mine, declares the Almighty Lord." Even though this story is a message to the Israelites, it applies to us as well. When we trust and believe in Jesus, we become wedded to Him. He covers us with forgiveness, kindness, goodness and love. He becomes the best of all providers to us, his wife.

Listen as the story becomes more interesting. Ezekiel 16: 9-14 (NLT): "Then I bathed you and washed off your blood, and I rubbed fragrant oils into your skin. I gave you expensive clothing of linen and silk, beautifully embroidered, and sandals made of fine leather. I gave you lovely jewelry, bracelets, and beautiful necklaces, a ring for your nose and earrings for your ears, and a lovely crown for your head. And so you were made beautiful with gold and silver. Your clothes were made of fine linen and were beautifully embroidered. You ate the finest foods--fine flour, honey, and olive oil--and became more beautiful than ever. You looked like a queen, and so you were! Your fame soon spread throughout the world on account of your beauty, because the splendor I bestowed on you perfected your beauty, says the Sovereign Lord." Father God treats us with the same care as he did this baby girl. He cleans us up and refreshes us. He gives us good things to enjoy, to wear, to adorn with. He loves beautiful things!

On with the story. Find out how she responds to God's kindness and goodness. Ezekiel 16:15-19 (GWT): "But you trusted your beauty, and you used your fame to become a prostitute. You had sex with everyone who walked by. You took some of your clothes and made your worship sites colorful. This is where you acted like a prostitute. Such things shouldn't happen. They shouldn't occur. You took your beautiful gold and silver jewelry that I had given you and made male idols for yourself. Then you committed adultery with them. You took off your embroidered clothes and covered the idols with them. You offered my olive oil and incense in their presence. You also offered them sweet and fragrant sacrifices. You gave flour, olive oil, and honey-- all the food that I gave you to eat. This is what happened, declares the Almighty Lord." The way we commit spiritual adultery is we listen to the world (magazines, infomercials, critics, etc.) instead of God. We take what others say and treat their words as special, treasures, words of wisdom. Our hearts become infatuated with their ideals instead of God's truth.

So, what's next? Ezekiel 16.59-63 (MSG): "God, the Master, says, I'll do to you just as you have already done, you who have treated my oath with contempt and broken the covenant. All the same, I'll remember the covenant I made with you when you were young and I'll make a new covenant with you that will last forever. You'll remember your sorry past and be properly contrite when you receive back your sisters, as participants in your covenant. I'll firmly establish my covenant with you and you'll know that I am God. You'll remember your past life and face the shame of it, but when I make atonement for you, make everything right after all you've done, it will leave you speechless. Decree of God, the Master." God is giving you a chance to redo your vows with him.

The great news is he will never, ever divorce you. He wants you back and all for himself. He loves you dearly, so much so he is willing to forgive your wondering away from him and receive you back, arms opened wide.

Beautiful or Ugly?

Do you consider yourself beautiful? Most of us don't. Some of us are afraid to claim beauty for fear of growing a bad kind of pride in ourselves. So, if you don't feel like you're beautiful then you must be ugly, right? Have you thought about what it means to be ugly? Ugly means: frightful, hideous, and offensive to the sight. Does that definition describe you? You may feel ugly but do people gasp in horror when you approach them?

Suppose you're a person who is obese, disfigured by fire, damaged by cancer, or just plain beat down by belittling attacks on social media. Some of these are fixable; some are not--at least not physically. Whatever shape you find yourself in at the moment, I urge you to face yourself in the mirror. God sees the same face you are looking at. But he sees you differently. You see yourself through eyes of an injured mind (soul) but God sees you as a healed person. The folks who treat you with horror do not represent him. They represent Satan. Satan has a reason for beating you down. He knows of God's good plans for you and is trying his best to keep you from fulfilling those good plans. Psalm 118:8 (TLB): "It is better to trust the Lord than to put confidence in men." Father has good plans even for souls like you who may not look the part. He loves to spring surprises on the least expecting ones.

What is Real Beauty?

What makes a person attractive or unattractive? A wide range of facial features and body shapes are pleasing to look at. Some people are drawn to a familiar look because it reminds them of a parent. So, who's to say what is attractive and what's not? What kind of person appears attractive to you? Everyone has a different opinion as to what beauty is, so would you say that beauty isn't what you once thought it was? Is beauty defined by a narrow margin or does it capture a broad range of possibilities?

I believe beauty is in the mind and not truly a visual thing. Listen to God's definition of beauty in 1 Samuel 16:7 (TLB):

"Don't judge by a man's face or height, for this is not the one. I don't make decisions the way you do! Men judge by outward appearance, but I look at a man's thoughts and intentions."

I'll be the first to admit that I judge a person's beauty by their facial features, clothes, popularity, etc. It's funny how we assign other things to a person's beauty that has nothing to do with the physical body. You could say it's a package deal. Indeed it is! All of us have the option of a good package deal with God! Take a look at a bad package deal found in Proverbs 11:22 (NCV): "A beautiful woman without good sense is like a gold ring in a pig's snout." She is the gold ring. Now imagine where the snout of a pig goes--it's not pleasant! I'd say the snout refers to our minds-- we go where our minds go.

My mind has traveled in some nasty places over the years. Kids made fun of my big nose when I was child. A have a small frame, including my chest area. This was pointed out to me in my teenage years, and believe it or not, it was an adult who mentioned it--consider the weight that comment carried. I was always self-conscious of a big birthmark on the front of my left calf. I heard words about my body and processed them in my mind. I made conclusions based on the knowledge I was given by my peers. I believed them when they pointed out my flaws.

I'm sure you have your own stories to tell about your body flaws. The next time you are among other people, turn and look at the one next to you. They have their stories, too! You are not the only one with flaws--all of us have them. It is Satan's desire to steal our worth, kill our confidence, and destroy our beautiful appearance. My answer to the lady who still thinks she looks fat is based on a lie from Satan. He knows you won't consult God's word to rewire your thinking--hence, you'll forever think you are fat and unusable by Father.

Psalm 45:11 (TLB) assures us that God intends for us to be beautiful: "Your royal husband delights in your beauty. Reverence him, for he is your Lord." But are you still hung up on the whole physical thing? Check out Jeremiah 17:9 (AMP): "The heart is deceitful above all things, and it is exceedingly perverse and corrupt and severely, mortally sick! Who can know it [perceive, understand, be acquainted with his own heart and mind]?" It's hard to swallow that we can't trust our own minds, but the lady who lies to herself about her weight is a good example. We all know someone who has lost weight but still looks at them self as fat--it could be you! Don't worry; the physical beauty thing is still a possibility!

You know by now that I have been mentally healed by God's word. How has it affected my beauty status? A while back, I haphazardly thought about myself. I was pleasantly surprised to hear myself say, "I like my body! It looks good! I feel comfortable and energetic in it." That thought freed me a bit more to go out and be a people person without worrying about my appearance. This wonderful phenomenon is talked about in 1 Peter 3:4 (TLB): "Be beautiful inside, in our hearts, with the lasting charm of a gentle and quiet spirit that is so precious to God." My spirit was quiet because I wasn't arguing between myself and God about my appearance.

Consider the verses where God gifts us with the task of displaying his splendor. Look up Isaiah 61:3(NIV). It's one of those verses. Gorgeous is another word for splendor. One of the verses we read earlier in this chapter speaks of it, Ezekiel 16:14 (NLT): "Your fame soon spread throughout the world because of your beauty. I dressed you in my splendor and perfected your beauty, says the Sovereign Lord."

Let's look at another side of beauty. There are some folks who are successful, energetic, and fun loving. They enjoy life, people and things. They are assertive and willing to try new things. You are drawn to them like a magnet. Then you do a double take and realize they are an average Joe or Jane. Yet, these people are beautiful souls (or minds). Is it possible to see someone as their mind instead of their outward appearance? That's how we see God and Jesus and Holy Spirit, why not people?

A person fitting the description from the last paragraph is living the new life. I believe Proverbs 3:26 (AMP) describes this type of beautiful person: "For the Lord shall be your confidence, firm and strong, and shall keep your foot from being caught [in a trap or some hidden danger]." Confidence is a mark of beauty, don't you agree? Hebrews 10:35 (Voice) challenges you to consider what you lose out on if you don't possess a quality of confidence: "Do not abandon your confidence, which will lead to rich rewards."

Look at the face of a confident person. You see a lovely smile. You won't see worry lines on this face. His/her eyes are bright and wide open. This person's spirit is engaging and friendly. She/he seems to know what to say and do. You want to be that person, don't you? You can be!

The definition of confidence is: a faith or belief that one will act in a right, proper, or effective way. That describes living life God's way. Faith and belief in God's word assures you of a confident manner. 1 John 5:14 (Voice) pictures you the way God sees you: "We live in the bold confidence that God hears our voices when we ask for things that fit His plan." His plan is for you to display His beauty and splendor. His plan is for you to be a confident person so that others would want what you have. His plan is for you to like your body and feel comfortable in it so you can stop having an internal argument with God. It is Father's plan for you to live abundantly and enjoy being you.

The confident person knows what his/her purpose is here on this earth. God has a purpose for your life and he wants you to know it, too. Ephesians 2:10 (from the beginning of this chapter) tells us that living life on purpose is a good thing. Listen to another version (CEB) of this verse: "We are God's accomplishment, created in Christ Jesus to do good things. God planned for these good things to be the way that we live our lives." Does your life represent God's accomplishment? That's a big responsibility, isn't it? You should take this confident/beautiful life thing seriously!

Friend, your mind may be filled with crazy stuff people have told you about your body. Be bold and turn off the crazy stuff. God is giving you permission, or rather, he's insisting, that you embrace the beautiful life that is already yours. Just read up on your life in the bible and enjoy it. Repeat over and over the good things Father says about you. Memorize verses that promote your beauty. Handwrite once a day for 21 days those scriptures that enhance your confidence and faith in Father.

One day you'll look in the mirror and say, "I like my body." "I am comfortable and energetic." "Life is beautiful!"

THE SURROUNDED LIFE

Chapter Eleven

There you are sitting in a comfy chair, sipping on a cup of coffee, while reading this book. Chances are you are in a quiet place and alone. But, are you really alone? Sounds spooky, doesn't it? Go ahead and look around. Do you see anyone else? Just because you don't see anyone--does it mean you are alone?

Don't close the book just yet. This chapter may prove challenging to you, but accept my challenge and keep on reading. It's my job to open your eyes to the unseen beings that live among us.

A Barna poll says that a majority of us Christians don't believe Satan exists. You may fall in the majority category. You may be a Christian who talks about other spirits but don't take them seriously. You may admit they exist but you don't think they affect you. Your dismissal-type attitude towards the spirits make them more dangerous to you.

We humans use the visual part of us to experience things. We feel we have to see something in order to believe it's real. Do we limit the possibilities of things not seen? Perhaps so.

What are the Unseen Beings?

That means we have to do a little research to prove the human-type experience wrong. The word "spirit" means wind and breath.

I discovered a funny thing while looking up the definitions of these three words. You'll find a connection of sorts between them. The word "wind" means breath and the word "breath" means a slight breeze, inhaled and exhaled air, as well as being a spirit.

Our research leads us to the bible. Notice the references of the wind and breath in our discovery verses. The first verse to learn from is Genesis 2:7 (MSG): "God formed Man out of dirt from the ground and blew into his nostrils the breath of life. The Man came alive--a living soul!" The connecting words in this verse are: "blew" as in wind and "breath." The most interesting part about this verse is what God's wind and breath created--"a living soul" or the spirit and mind of man. A study note in The Voice translations says: "When human body meets divine spirit, a soul is born." Remember that God held a lifeless form of human before he breathed into it. Imagine the shell of a body without a mind. This phenomenon happened here at the creation of human, and it happened when Mary became pregnant with Jesus, and it happens again when we get saved. Jesus promised us new life and he gives it to us as spoken in John 20:22 (GWT): "After he had said this, he breathed on the disciples and said, 'Receive the Holy Spirit.'" Jesus performed this new-birth event on the disciples after he was resurrected to new life himself.

Old Mind, New Mind

You may be wondering what the difference is between a new-life soul (mind) and an old-life soul (mind). Listen as Jesus teaches us the difference in John 3:8 (Voice): "The wind blows all around us as if it has a will of its own; we feel and hear it, but we do not understand where it has come from or where it will end up. Life in the Spirit is as if it were the wind of God." A new-life mind is infused with Holy Spirit. A quick review of Chapter Two, The Enriched Life, reminds us that we stop being a "me" and become a "we." An old-life mind can will itself to be good but a new-life mind has Holy Spirit nudging us and helping us to be and do good and giving us beyond-human strength and powers. I believe the last sentence of John 3:8, "Life in the Spirit is as if it were the wind of God," refers to the mind of God. I believe this because The Spirit is breath and breath is also wind. God blew (as in wind) breath into the human and created a soul. God birthed our soul out of his soul. God has a mind, you know. He is all knowing. He is the one who teaches us.

Father uses our minds to grow us up as taught in Ephesians 4:14 (NLT): "Then we will no longer be immature like children. We won't be tossed and blown about by every wind of new teaching. We will not be influenced when people try to trick us with lies so clever they sound like truth." Notice the reference of wind as being a vehicle for teaching. The new teaching in this case refers to bad teaching, lies and falsehoods meant to blow us off God's path.

The Hebrew word "ruach" and the Greek word "pneuma" are the bible words for our English word "spirit." The ruach and pneuma refer to wind, breath, human emotion, human understanding, will power and life itself. Do you see references to your mind in their definitions? The word "spirit" is interchanged for soul but I believe we get the two confused because they connect to each other. The soul (mind) is human and the spirit is where God lives in us. He wants to influence us (mind) but we usually resist the spirit part of us. If we resist the Spirit of God living in us then what happens by default?

James 1:6 (Voice) answers the question in the last paragraph: "The key is that your request be anchored by your single-minded commitment to God. Those who depend only on their own judgment are like those lost on the seas, carried away by any wave or picked up by any wind." Notice what happens to those who depend on their own judgment (mind). That person chooses to open him/herself up to other influences, influences that aren't God. Did you catch who the last word, wind, was pointing at? It wasn't God.

Unseen Beings

Are you convinced yet that spirits are among us? If not, allow 2 Corinthians 4:18 (CEB) to convince you: "We don't focus on the things that can be seen but on the things that can't be seen. The things that can be seen don't last, but the things that can't be seen are eternal." This verse is referring to material things in our lives as well as our bodies. These things are visible yet they do not last forever. Our minds and spirits will last forever, whether they are with God or with Satan. You see, our minds are housed in bodies that will die off but our minds don't die. Our minds can live outside our bodies (once they die) and are able to live in heaven or hell.

Some people believe that Christians cannot be possessed by an evil spirit. Well, let's take a deeper look at what it means to be possessed. Webster says that possession means a psychological state in which an individual's normal personality is replaced by another. How many times have you felt overtaken by anxiety and fear? A rage of anger can come out of nowhere when the key issue isn't resolved. They call jealousy a green-eyed monster. Have you ever been labeled insanely jealous? Isolation is a trait of a depressed person. Do you get out and enjoy God's good earth and people and show-off God to others? If you don't then you're drowning in despair. What did John 10:10 say about Satan? Oh, he steals kills and destroys lives.

A person can be possessed in different forms and levels. A person can be possessed by an evil spirit bodily, mentally, emotionally or intellectually. Possession ranges from being influenced to being owned. Controlled and dominated are other words used in place of possession. We Christians like to use the word "stronghold" when referring to a battle with a bad trait because we find that word in the bible, but we don't like the word possession. Guess what a stronghold is? It is domination by a particular group or characteristic. The "group" could certainly mean "unclean spirits."

Consider where the stronghold (or domination) takes place. 2 Corinthians 10:4 (NLT) sheds light on where it happens: "We use God's mighty weapons, not worldly weapons, to knock down the strongholds of human reasoning and to destroy false arguments." Umm. I guess it occurs in the mind. Verse 5b (NLT) tells us how to fight against the unclean spirits: "We are taking prisoners of every thought, every emotion, and subduing them into obedience to the Anointed One." The battle takes place in the mind and it is won in the mind. Psalm 9:9 (NIV) explains this phenomenon: "The Lord is a refuge for the oppressed, a stronghold in times of trouble." Notice a flip-flop of the stronghold.

How to Get Rid of Unclean Spirits

Remember how I said an old-life mind can force himself to do good but that it doesn't last? Jesus explains how this happens in Matthew 12:43-45 (TLB): "The evil nation is like a man possessed by a demon. For if the demon leaves, it goes into the deserts for a while, seeking rest but finding none. Then it says, 'I will return to the man I came from.' So it returns and finds the man's heart clean but empty! Then the demon finds seven other spirits more evil than itself, and all enter the man and live in him. And so he is worse off than before." Two words jump out at me, "empty" and "heart." I wondered how a man's heart can be empty. The problem with man forcing himself to be good (and temporarily forcing out the evil spirits) is that at that moment in time he is empty. He doesn't have anything in him giving him purpose and value. Even bad spirits give a purpose and value, albeit, the wrong kind.

Ecclesiastes 3:11 (NLV) gives more detail about the heart (mind): "He has made everything beautiful in its time. He has put thoughts of the forever in man's mind, yet man cannot understand the work God has done from the beginning to the end." Whether you are an old-life mind or a new-life mind, your mind knows it will live on forever, somewhere. God planted this forever mentality in our minds. We may deny that this hard-to-believe thought exists in us, but it does. Things begin to make sense when you accept this special truth about us.

Mark 1:23 (GWT) alludes to the fact that disturbed people are found in church: "At that time there was a man in the synagogue who was controlled by an evil spirit." It's no wonder that you find people who are struggling with issues in the church. They are searching for relief and healing. Don't you go to church seeking help with your issues? Ephesians 5: 15-17 (Voice) tells us that overcoming unclean spirits happens outside the walls of the church, too: "So be careful how you live; be mindful of your steps. Don't run around like idiots as the rest of the world does. Instead, walk as the wise! Make the most of every living and breathing moment because these are evil times. So understand and be confident in God's will, and don't live thoughtlessly."

The prescription is the same whether a person is affected by an unclean spirit bodily, mentally, emotionally, or intellectually. The man in the synagogue was thrown into a convulsion when he met up with Jesus. The prescription for this man and for you is found in Mark 1:27 (GWT): "Everyone was stunned. They said to each other, 'What is this? This is a new teaching that has authority behind it! He gives orders to evil spirits, and they obey him.'"

Jesus' spoken word as well as the written word is the key to wellness. Read Hebrews 4:12 (AMP) slowly: "For the Word that God speaks is alive and full of power [making it active, operative, energizing, and effective]; it is sharper than any two-edged sword, penetrating to the dividing line of the breath of life (soul) and [the immortal] spirit, and of joints and marrow [of the deepest parts of our nature], exposing and sifting and analyzing and judging the very thoughts and purposes of the heart." In other words, God's words target the very place that Satan attacks--the mind. Another thing or two to take note of is what didn't happen when Jesus told the unclean spirit to get out of the man: no exorcism, no shock treatment, no biofeedback, and no group therapy. Jesus simply spoke firm, authoritative words to the minds of the unclean spirits.

I recently read a Facebook post and was intrigued by her words of despair. Listen to some of her phrases: "Losing my mind." "I am succumbing to the tough stuff." "I am at a low emotional point." "I have lost my way." "I am overwhelmed with emotions." "I am utterly desperate and completely alone." "I don't have the ability to pull myself out of this darkness." "I found myself curled up in a ball, tears streaming down my cheeks, on the verge of having a panic attack." Dear reader, do any of these statements of being overcome by unclean spirits match your statements? Now listen to the end of her post: "As I was curled up in a ball I heard God's small voice speak to me--'remember the significance of Easter.' An indescribable peace immediately overcame me." My Facebook friend was made mentally well by God's words in her thoughts. She heard his words, obeyed his words (by remembering the significance of Easter) and was given relief of her torture.

The Good and The Bad

In the beginning God, Jesus and Holy Spirit created the heavens and the earth. They created everything on the earth including us humans. Let's travel backwards in time. The angels were created before we were. Angels are similar to us humans as they have personalities, features and personal abilities and assignments. The bible records names of several of them. But one of them, namely Lucifer, changed his life and our lives forever.

Lucifer was the most beautiful and strongest of all the angels. He was given the position as the top angel. The name "Lucifer" as translated in the Hebrew language, means "daystar, son of the morning and bringer of the dawn. It is in my opinion that Lucifer was honored with the gift of his name.

We were created to have a relationship with God, to honor him and be loyal to him. So, too, the angels were created to worship and honor God. We were created with a human body. The angels are spiritual beings. Humans cannot become an angel. The major difference between us and angels is the fact that we have bodies that die. Angels do not have bodies that die. Hebrews 2:9 (GWT) states a curious fact: "Jesus was made a little lower than the angels." Our physical condition that leads to death makes us (and Jesus while here on earth as a human) lower than the angels. But 1 Corinthians 6:3 (TLB) explains how this circumstance flip-flops: "Don't you realize that we Christians will judge and reward the very angels in heaven?" The flip-flop takes place after we enter heaven. Something that doesn't flip-flop is our shared allegiance to God. Different roles, but same importance.

You can find the story of the top angel, Lucifer, in Ezekiel 28:12-18 and Isaiah 14:12-15. I encourage you to look these stories up because they paint a fascinating picture of the top angel. His history reveals him to have been the most beautiful creature ever to have existed. Even Lucifer was amazed at his own strength and authority. His amazement grew into an over inflated ego. He took his eyes and loyalty off of God and onto himself. It's important for you to realize that angels, including Lucifer, have minds and can think. It was ok for Lucifer to recognize his beauty but it wasn't ok for him to dwell on it too long. That's how sin was born. That's why self-indulgence is hard-wired in us. This sin grew into rebellion. Lucifer decided he could take on God and become god. Boy, was he wrong. He may have been the number one angel but he doesn't recognize that he will never be number one god.

His sin changed his life forever. He lost his prestigious position, his garden home, his beautiful appearance, and even his name. Revelation 12:9 (TLB) reveals his new name, new position, new face, new band of angels and new home: "This great Dragon-- the ancient serpent called the devil, or Satan, the one deceiving the whole world--was thrown down onto the earth with all his army." His new job is to oversee his band of angels. It is their job to lie to us, cheat us out of a good life and lead us down the wrong path, away from God. They hate God and don't want anyone to follow God. Strangely, after all of Satan's changes, he still believes he can be top god.

I've often wondered how Satan could think he could overthrow the Almighty God. The bible tells us that God knows everything, is everywhere at all times, has all authority, and has unlimited power. Satan pales in contrast. Satan doesn't know everything. He isn't everywhere all the time--that's why he needs his demon helpers to be out and about. He doesn't have all authority but he achieves some authority when we give in to him. Satan has some power but not unlimited power. It's probably true that Satan lies to himself about his shortcomings that prevent him from being the top god.

John 8:44 (GWT) exposes Satan's disregard for the truth: "You come from your father, the devil, and you desire to do what your father wants you to do. The devil was a murderer from the beginning. He has never been truthful. He doesn't know what the truth is. Whenever he tells a lie, he's doing what comes naturally to him. He's a liar and the father of lies." We find Jesus in a conversation with his accusers. Jesus told them that their actions and words reflected their spiritual father, the devil. Why do you think Jesus calls the devil a murderer from the beginning? Jude 1:6 (AMP) sheds light on the beginning part: "And angels who did not keep (care for, guard, and hold to) their own first place of power but abandoned their proper dwelling place--these He has reserved in custody in eternal chains (bonds) under the thick gloom of utter darkness until the judgment and doom of the great day!" Satan murdered himself and the angels who followed him. He also murders anyone who believes his lies and follow him to hell.

Satan, the father of lies, rejected the source of truth, God. It's funny how he hates God but he is afraid of him. Check out James 2:19 (Voice): "Do you think that just believing there's one God is going to get you anywhere? The demons believe that, too, and it terrifies them!" A large number of people have the wool pulled over their minds' eyes. They think the act of believing in God is enough for salvation--but if that were true, why are the demons so terrified of God? You see, the demons don't want you to go any further than knowing God exists. Our faith and trust in God goes deeper than face value. Faith in God is like an energy drink. It propels one to be activated. James 2:24 (Voice) says: "We are made right with God through good works, not simply by what we believe or think." Satan will tell you all day long that you're ok with just acknowledging that God is real, but he doesn't want you to commit to God.

Satan uses a small amount of truth in order to trick you. He does it all the time. He is committed to his efforts per 2 Corinthians 11:14 (NLT): Even Satan disguises himself as an angel of light." He uses a pseudo hope, or the light at the end of the tunnel, as a tool. He knows we Christians are lazy and not as alert as the bible warns us to be and he takes advantage of us. He baits us with dabs of truth and we don't notice the deception that follows.

I've been listening to sermons on TV as part of my research for this chapter. I listened attentively for words of truth. One minister preached about God's favor and how he wants to elevate us. This statement is true. But the rest of the sermon was about human elevation. Because I love Jesus so dearly, I get a thrill anytime I hear his name and praises of him. I did not get one single zing out of the sermon. This preacher spoke of the bible but didn't read from it. He spoke of God as the one who can elevate us but not a word of elevation for our great God. I felt like God was being used and not worshipped. And wouldn't you know that this minister has one of the largest congregations in America---a very big wool over many eyes.

Life Study

Satan and his evil spirits know you quite well. But they only know you through observation. They learn how to manipulate you. They've watched you react to certain words and events. They have watched humans for thousands of years and know how circumstances create certain behaviors and weaken human spirits. He knows what scares you and what angers you.

The devil knows that we hinge our worth on the opinions of people instead of God. We treat people as gods. What does God say about idols? The Old Testament is full of commands to not worship idols. Jesus says in the New Testament that no one can come to the Father except through Him.

Satan loves it when we cling to the victim status, throw a pity party, become hyped up by anxiety and treat obsessions as personality traits. He knows you are vulnerable when you make statements such as, "I was born this way," "I don't have control over my thoughts," and "No one loves me." He recognizes that these statements are not connected to God. You, too, should learn to recognize that these statements are not connected to God.

You are following down Satan's path if you still aren't certain he exists. He loves leading you down dark, dank paths. Speaking of paths, did you know that the beliefs in karma, fate and destiny are the opposite of believing in God? Karma is a word taken from eastern religions of Hinduism and Buddhism. Karma is small-truth trickery. Notice the similarity in God's word found in Matthew 7:2a (Voice): "For you will be treated as you treat others."

Fate is the belief that something causes events to happen. It conveniently doesn't point to God, but it points to just something. Colossians 1:16 (Voice) points directly to God: "It was by him that everything was created: the heavens, the earth, all things within and upon them, all things seen and unseen, thrones and dominions, spiritual powers and authorities. Every detail was crafted through his design, by His own hands, and for His purposes."

People crave to know their destiny--and truly God put that desire in us. But a person gets on the wrong track when they search for any kind of power that can outline a predetermined course of life events. Consider how there is a tug-of-war with the plans for a person's life. Look no farther because God has your life already planned out as spoken of in Jeremiah 29:11 (NIRV): "I know the plans I have for you, announces the Lord. I want you to enjoy success. I do not plan to harm you. I will give you hope for the years to come." God's plans sound like something you'd like, don't you agree?

How Unclean Spirits Invade Us

I recently spent a couple of days with a group of people known to have angry personalities. By day two, I found myself agitated and restless. I took some time away from them and recited my power verses (core 20 memory verses). But I was troubled (which isn't an emotion from God) that when I returned I wasn't any better. I asked God why this happened to me. He made me think about the story in Matthew 17: 14-20. The disciples had been successfully driving out demons until a man approached them with his son. The son was violently tortured by a demon, causing convulsions and throwing him into fire and water. The disciples asked Jesus why they failed this time. Jesus told them (Matthew 17:20a AMP); "Because of the littleness of your faith [that is, your lack of firmly relying trust]." I was still stumped how I was overtaken by a mysterious force. Then I read the rest of verse 20:

"For truly I say to you, if you have faith [that is living] like a grain of mustard seed, you can say to this mountain, Move from here to yonder place, and it will move; and nothing will be impossible to you." I discovered that my faith had wilted, or died a little. I would have had success had I prayed about the situation before going to be with this group. The fact is, our past issues had been resolved and I didn't recognize the need to pray about it this time. Boy was I wrong, tricked is more like it.

My agitation caused me to be open (because I thought things were ok between us) and mention how hurt I was because of an inconsideration on the part of one of them. Wow, an explosion blew up in my face. I admit that it was my fault and eventually we all apologized, but the explosion (past and present) are etched in my mind. That's exactly why my faith died a little while being there. I mentally gave more power to the anger than I did to God.

Anger is a good example of how unclean spirits work in a person's life. The bible warns us in Psalm 4:4 (NLV): "Shake with anger and do not sin. When you are on your bed, look into your hearts and be quiet." Anger by itself is not something wrong to feel. It becomes a problem when you allow it to grow and fester. This verse tells us to get by ourselves, in quietness, and think about what we are angry about--in other words, deal with it, don't let your feelings grow. Deal with it by talking to God about it and getting direction from him about how to deal with the situation. By the way, this prescription applies to fear, jealousy, anxiety, depression, etc. Verse 5 says to trust the Lord, hence, listen to his advice and do what he says to do. Ephesians 4:26 (TLB) expresses the wrong way to treat personal anger: "If you are angry, don't sin by nursing your grudge. Don't let the sun go down with you still angry--get over it quickly." Again, deal with it, with God. Verse 27 (NLV) explains what happens when we don't deal with it: "Do not let the devil start working in your life."

Listen to the bible's advice about being around people known to be angry, Proverbs 22:24 (ERV) says: "Don't be friends with people who become angry easily. Don't stay around quick-tempered people." Verse 25 (ERV) tells why: "If you do, you may learn to be like them. Then you will have the same problems they do." I'm learning from this passage that my mind was weak and vulnerable from past experiences. Things would have been different if I had talked to God about the visit before going and allowed him to be in control.

One more thought about angry people. Listen to Proverbs 29:22 (ERV): "An angry person causes arguments, and someone who is quick-tempered is guilty of many sins." It seems that anger leads to other bad behaviors. Anger lives in us (unclean spirits) as long as we nurse them, but they move out when we allow God to send them out. We have to let go of the pain and give it to God.

Jesus Knows You

There's a difference in the way Jesus knows you and how Satan knows you. Satan didn't know you existed until you were born. Jeremiah 1:5 tells us that Jesus knows about us before he created us in our mother's womb. Satan had to study you and your habits. Jesus chose you before he created the world (Ephesians 1:4). Satan wants to diminish you and be able to use you. Jesus has a special work for you to do in order to serve him.

Satan baited you so that you would choose his influence. Jesus didn't wait for you to choose him. He chose you first and has a special assignment for you (John 15:16).

Satan wants you to hinge your worth on the opinions of people. God wants you to hinge your worth on him (Galatians 1:10). Satan wants you to remain captive to his services. Jesus tells you that you are free from Satan's captivity. Jesus is releasing you from the darkness of your prison cell. Jesus is healing your broken-hearted wounds (Isaiah 61:1).

Satan keeps you unsatisfied and always searching for love (in all the wrong places and with the wrong people). John 14:23 (GWT) offers a rebuttal: "Jesus answered him, 'Those who love me will do what I say. My Father will love them, and we will go to them and make our home with them.'" Consider that God's love (not self-love) makes you feel accepted and worthy and at home. Satan knows that an on-going close relationship with Jesus builds barriers up to keep Satan and his demons away from you.

Ask Jesus to reveal himself to you, to make him more real. Relate to Jesus in a real-time fashion. Don't just talk about him or think about him. Talk to him, think thoughts to him. Grow that relationship! You'll be growing your real self when you do.

Buy This and You'll be Happy

Are you aware that all advertisements are produced with the

intent to make you feel unhappy with your life? Their goal is to persuade you to buy their products with the promise that you'll be happy once you make the purchase. Companies use psychology to sell their products. They play mind games with you. They play these games for their profit advantage and against your reasoning abilities. Satan uses the same kind of tricks on your mind.

Satan targets your mind in order to do his work. Think back on the anger section. Anger leads to more sin. Unlike the market, Satan isn't looking to grow his kingdom, because he doesn't love you--he only loves himself. His aim is to shrink God's kingdom. He accomplishes this by tricking you into thinking his thoughts. Check out Romans 8:6 (NCV): "But if people's thinking is controlled by the sinful self, there is death. But if their thinking is controlled by the Spirit, there is life and peace." Selfish thoughts are a product of Satan's prideful thoughts of wanting to be number one god. This verse confirms that having our thoughts controlled by Satan brings about death--mental death, which can lead to physical death--ranging from depression to suicide. Note the contrast of thinking Holy Spirit thoughts: good mental health and enjoyable life experiences.

If you were to return to Genesis 3, you'd discover that Satan didn't twist Eve's arm to make her sin. He merely twisted the truth into a false belief. She took the bait because she liked the way he thought. She bought what he was selling.

I did a research on the religion (that's hard to type) of Satanism. Before I read up on it, my mind imagined people bowing down to Satan, sacrificing animals to him, and chanting mantras of praise for his ways. But imagine my surprise to find out the main purpose of this religion is to elevate oneself or self-promotion. It doesn't seem to be about him at all (but oh, does he have folks fooled!). The pursuit of individualism is pushed. These acts create a pre-occupation with oneself.

Preoccupation with oneself isn't a hard sell. It just needs a little nudge. I'm afraid that's why tens of thousands of people flock to Christian-type churches that sell Satan's way of thinking. 1 Timothy 4:1 (TLB) rejects my fears: "But the Holy Spirit tells us clearly that in the last times some in the church will turn away from Christ and become eager followers of teachers with devil-inspired ideas." Remember the preacher I told you about who elevated people but not God? This was a well-known Christian-type church. It seems that these types of preachers take a grain of truth about grace and mercy and twist them into falsehood. I'm sure lots of people become interested in the bible with the sole intent of learning how to elevate themselves using those grains of truth and ignoring the whole truth about grace and mercy. They fail to elevate our great God. These sad tens of thousands of people have not only bought what Satan was selling but they sold their souls (minds) to him. Mark 8:36 (TLB) confirms it: "And how does a man benefit if he gains the whole world and loses his soul in the process?"

Another thing Satan sells is the idea of getting personal information and guidance from the occult world. People are hungry to know what their purpose is in the world but don't consider the underlying elements of the occult. The word "occult" means to be secret and to conceal. That definition is in reference to deception and hiding the truth. Mediums, horoscopes and séances are from evil sources. God warns us about them in Leviticus 19:31 (GWT): "Don't turn to psychics or mediums to get help. That will make you unclean. I am the Lord your God." Did you notice the mention of unclean spirits? Father wants you to get your help and life information from him. Now that you know this information, what will you do when tempted the next time by one of those sources? Trust God with future endeavors--I promise you, he'll satisfy you. Ask him anything and you'll hear from him.

Satan can sell you a self-promotion product in a back-door fashion. Some of us suffer from bad events that have caused us embarrassment, guilt-ridden shame, and haunting fear--that causes us to keep the event a secret. Secrets make us feel isolated, even from God. Because we feel so alone, we feel we have to become our own savior. My dear friend, you can never be separated from God (Romans 8:38-29). You might be surprised to know that God can read your thoughts. Psalm 139:2b (TLB): When far away you know my every thought." And verse 4 (TLB) says this: "You know what I am going to say before I even say it." Now, soak in the truth about your thoughts found in Psalm 94:11 (NLT): "The Lord knows people's thoughts; he knows they are worthless." Hmm. That means you shouldn't trust you own thoughts. Only God-thoughts are right and good and healthy. So, go ahead and talk to God about that embarrassing situation and get it resolved so you can really live.

Along the line of back-door salesman, Satan sells you a lie saying that another person is more attractive than you, smarter and more successful than you. That other person seems to be perfect and you aren't. God reveals to us what the root of jealousy is in James 3:15 (NLT): "For jealousy and selfishness are not God's kind of wisdom. Such things are earthly, unspiritual, and demonic." Did you notice how jealousy and selfishness are coupled together? And how about the finger pointing to demons?

Do you have a problem being suppressed by shame and guilt, being unable to resolve it? Guilt is not meant to be held onto. Your advise is from an unclean spirit. Holy Spirit wants you to admit the wrongful act, turn away from it, release it to God and move forward. Jesus reveals Satan's persistence in the lie of guilt in Revelation 12:10b (NIRV): "Satan, who brings charges against our brothers and sisters, has been thrown down. He brings charges against them in front of our God day and night." He specifically targets us.

Other back-door purchases are: depression, anxiety, fear and anger. Depression is caused by feelings and thoughts of hopelessness. The person who buys depression becomes lethargic and isolated. Sounds like mental death to me. Anxiety is a hard thing to let go because of the addictive nature of the hormones that hype a person up. Unfortunately, the anxiety person has bought a crazy, chaotic mind. 2 Timothy 1:7 and Proverbs 30:33 states that fear and anger are impulse buys from demonic forces.

Salvation is Still the Answer

It's ironic that a lot of people don't recognize that Satan and his demons exist just as the Jews don't recognize that Jesus is our Spiritual savior. The Jews, both in bible times and today, are awaiting a man who will be a political leader, one who will set up a kingdom of peace, contentment and prosperity. People want peace, contentment and prosperity but only through self-promotion so they can serve themselves.

Jesus was sent to rescue us from Satan and his demons. He was sent to rehab us from the havoc Satan has created for us. Ephesians 6:11-17 outlines the steps we can take to stand up to Satan. Ephesians 6:11 (NIRV) tells us to: "Put on all of God's armor; then you can remain strong against the devil's plans." I admit to having an unhealthy fear of Satan in the past. While growing up I heard lots of sermons about spiritual warfare. It sounded scary to me. It didn't help that I lived in a military town and heard about wars and rumor of wars, along with the sounds of wargames. So, when I would read the antidote of spiritual warfare the words didn't click for me.

It could be that I got muddled up in all the war words. When reading Ephesians 6:11-17 I would get caught up with the pieces of armor instead of the spiritual tools they symbolized. Hmmm, I bought into Satan's trick. When I remove the actual weapons and concentrate on the spiritual ones--then I can grasp the antidote. Here they are: God's truth and approval. Faith and salvation. The Word of God and communication with God. Ephesians 6:12 (TLB) gives us a "most-wanted" picture of the enemy: "For we are not fighting against people made of flesh and blood, but against persons without-bodies--the evil rulers of the unseen world, those mighty satanic beings and great evil princes of darkness who rule this world; against huge numbers of wicked spirits in the spirit world."

I'm not sure why salvation is not the first one to be mentioned, but it's a very important element in our spiritual warfare. Salvation combats two things: sin and evil. Sin is the result of a human choice. Evil is the act of Satan and his demons. John 3:17 (AMP) offers us a promise: "For God did not send the Son into the world in order to judge (to reject, to condemn, to pass sentence on) the world, but that the world might find salvation and be made safe and sound through Him." As it turns out, my fear of spiritual warfare was blown out of proportion. Sure, it will happen, but Jesus has given me the tools I need to keep me safe and protected. I believe the more my faith and trust grows in this area the heavier the protection.

Jesus reminds us in Luke 10:20 (GWT) the importance of living out our salvation every day: "However, don't be happy that evil spirits obey you. Be happy that your names are written in heaven." You know, Jesus wouldn't have told us that the evil spirits will obey us (when we use his words) if it weren't true. But he does warn us to use this gift in times of need. Don't get caught up in the fact that you have unusual powers over the evil spirits. What you should get caught up in is the fact that you have a new life!

That brings me back to the reason I wrote this book, Biblical Mental Rehab. Mental Rehab can be achieved through Jesus

Christ. Be happy and rejoice in 2 Corinthians 5:17 (TLB): "When someone becomes a Christian, he becomes a brand new person inside. He is not the same anymore. A new life has begun!" Notice that the new life starts you-know-where, in the mind. Purge the unclean spirits from your mind and become new again!

THE GARDEN LIFE

Chapter Twelve

Have you noticed how popular it is to eat outdoors at restaurants? It is truly a treat to eat alfresco and the restaurants are capitalizing on its popularity. It seems that dining outdoors is relaxing and therapeutic. A garden experience reduces stress and improves concentration. Psychologists say that spending time in a garden improves our quality of life because we focus on the sights, sounds, and smells of the garden while mentally letting go of the frenzied pace of life.

I have a curiosity question. Why do we feel so relaxed and peaceful in a garden setting? Did you know that hospitals design and install "healing gardens?" These gardens are meant to meet physical, psychological, social and spiritual needs. One person claimed on a blog that she experienced the Divine while in her garden. I believe gardens are effective simply because we enjoy God (his creation), however, we don't realize it is God we are enjoying. His presence is felt in the beauty he created. I enjoy listening to the birds sing, the branches sway, and the fragrance of newly mown grass. It is an experience, a God experience. Enjoying God's beauty is an act of worship. He wants us to see Him in everything good. There is a rhythm felt in his creation. I'm reminded of his rhythm in Matthew 11: 30 (MSG): "Learn the unforced rhythms of grace. I won't lay anything heavy or ill-fitting on you. Keep company with me and you'll learn to live freely and lightly." Doesn't "freely and lightly" sound gardenish?

The Beginning

The garden life is the first living experience for the human race. The Garden of Eden was Adam and Eve's first home. Imagine living in a garden. I, personally, love gardens and plants. I love the lushness of tropical plants and the beauty of exotic flowers. Take a mental look at what Adam and Eve lived in every day. Fruit trees adorned with balls of red, yellow and orange. Bushes having berries of all colors hanging from their branches. Vines flowing down to the ground giving them shade. A garden is a delight to the eyes, ears, and nose. Adam and Eve had the privilege of living in the Garden day and night.

Adam and Eve enjoyed plentifulness. They had access to every fruit and vegetable grown in the Garden, except, of course, one tree. They felt free and light in this environment. Breezes swayed the limbs of the weeping willow trees. No doubt, they enjoyed eating the fruit while sitting on a carpet of soft, green grass, with no ants bothering them.

God was the first being they had a relationship with. He was their daddy. Adam and Eve knew that he created all of the wonderfulness they enjoyed living in. Life was very good for the couple.

I believe God intends to replant the Garden of Eden on the New Earth. It will be as perfect and breath taking as the first one. We will all enjoy living in the Garden just as Adam and Eve did, in fact, they'll be there, too!

The Good News is that you don't have to wait until the New Earth to enjoy living the garden life. Peter explains how this is true in 1 Peter 1:3-4 (MSG): "Because Jesus was raised from the dead, we've been given a brand-new life and have everything to live for, including a future in heaven--and the future starts now!" This old earth will be given new life just as we are given new life; however, we get a jump-start on our new life. The earth/garden will have to wait for its proper time to reappear.

I am saddened that some folks use the future heaven as a way of escape. They hate their life on this earth and can't wait to end it. They don't accept Father's healing and his restorative wellbeing. That way of living (or not living) is an unbiblical way of thinking, acting and living. Jesus died so that we can have abundant life, not a life that needs to be escaped from. Just because you're not feeling the abundant life or seeing the possibility of it doesn't mean it's not a reality.

2 Corinthians 5:5 (MSG) tells us how to use our longing for the heaven life during this present life: "The Spirit of God whets our appetite by giving us a taste of what's ahead. He puts a little of heaven in our hearts so that we'll never settle for less." Father wants us to experience a little of heaven now because he is already living in us. We don't have to wait until heaven to live with him or to experience his goodness.

When we are saved, we are given eternity, that is, living forever. But we tend to live as if the gift of eternity is yet to be given. We act and live as if we haven't received the benefit of salvation yet. I like the quote from an unknown author: "A little faith will bring your soul to heaven, but a lot of faith will bring heaven to your soul." This quote reminds me of 1 Timothy 4:8 (AMP): "For physical training is of some value (useful for a little), but godliness (spiritual training) is useful and of value in everything and in every way, for it holds promise for the present life and also for the life which is to come." Our lives to come are a continuation from our current lives.

So, how does faith help us to enjoy the garden life now? Faith and trust are connected with devotion and loyalty. You could say that love is fueled by faith and faith is fueled by love. Hebrews 11:1 (TLB) is saturated in love: "What is faith? It is the confident assurance that something we want is going to happen. It is the certainty that what we hope for is waiting for us, even though we cannot see it up ahead."

Some of us may have the wrong impression of what the garden life is like. We gravitate towards the feelings of peacefulness and quietness, enjoyment of beauty and relief of stress. We see ourselves lounging around with nothing to do but rest.

But consider the activity Father planned for us in the original Garden. The animals were named and tended to. Crops were planted and harvested. Relationships were cultivated and nourished. Activity and rest coexisted then and it can now. No activity is dead activity. A garden is a living thing that is growing. The garden life is also a living and growing thing.

Some of us are used to a dumpster life. Everything about our lives feels broken, twisted, and dirty. God doesn't want us to live in the dumpster. Our lives belong to Him. Get God out of the dumpster. As a saved person, you have been given a free ticket to heaven (which starts now). A dumpster life is not included in the price of the ticket. A new life is yours, free and clear. Just live it!

Go Back to the New Beginning

Human relationships started in the first Garden, the old beginning. Our relationship with God starts in the new beginning. My main fear in the past has been that of relationships. I was fearful of rejection, abandonment and put-downs. My idea of relationship was of fearfulness and pain. I had no idea that relationships were meant to be enjoyed. Just imagine how badly romantic love turns out for the person who has relationship-phobia. Relationships and love are learned behaviors. Faulty love behaviors can be unlearned. The bible teaches us how to learn the correct way. It's called the New Beginning. The New Beginning is a new agreement with God after Jesus came to earth.

The New Beginning is found in Luke 10:27 (ERV): "Love the Lord your God with all your heart, all your soul, all your strength, and all your mind. Love your neighbor the same as you love yourself." Jesus tells us in verse 28 (NLT): "Do this and you will live!" I talked about this verse in a small group at church not too long ago. A teacher admitted that it is hard to love God. Why does it seem so hard to love God? It could be because of poor relationship models in our young lives. You may not love God because you can't feel his love for you. Some people readily admit that their past sins make their love tainted. These folks feel unlovable.

Love is a two-way street. There is no such thing as a one-sided relationship. If you find yourself refusing (or feeling unable) to love God then I suggest you ask him to help you love him and ask him to help you to want to love him. 1 John 4:16 (NLT) is a perfect example of a relationship with God: "We know how much God loves us, and we have put our trust in Him. God is love, and all who love live in God and God lives in them." If you are a Christian, remember that you are a "we" and not a "me." Start telling yourself what the bible says about you. You have God's love and power in you (2 Timothy 1:7). Court God. Date Jesus. Hold hands with Holy Spirit. Get to know them. You'll feel their presence all the time instead of having to go to church to feel them.

Loving God reduces stress. Your decision-making becomes easier and smarter. Relationships start and grow and rekindle. You become more secure in being you. A strange thing happens. Your love for God allows you to back off and keep your mouth shut when in a relationship challenge. You're ok with who you are and God is ok with who you are. Why not love God the way he wants you to? What do you have to lose? What do you have to gain?

God's Reality

You may be living a dumpster life, but that's not God's plan for you. The dumpster life is Satan's plan for your life. But don't worry. The only change you need to make is to start loving God. Listen to James' advise in James 2:5 (MSG): "Listen, dear friends. Isn't it clear by now that God operates quite differently? He chose the world's down-and-out as the Kingdom's first citizens, with full rights and privileges. The kingdom is promised to anyone who loves God."

God created us humans to grow, prosper and mature. The bible tells how he super-sized lots of people, people like Abraham, Moses, and King David. Listen to God's words to you in Isaiah 43:19 (MSG): "Be alert, be present. I'm about to do something brand-new. It's bursting out! Don't you see it? There it is! I'm making a road through the desert, rivers in the badlands." Do you recognize your dumpster life as the badlands? What did he tell you to do? Go back and read it again. He wants you to live in the present and be alert to the here and now. Mentally leave the things that are troubling you behind. Travel forward with God. Get out of the dumpster and enter the garden.

You may be wondering what to do with the garbage. You may feel like your garbage life has been a sacrifice. So offer it to God as a sacrifice of praise. Hebrews 13:15 (ERV): "So through Jesus we should never stop offering our sacrifice to God. That sacrifice is our praise, coming from lips that speak his name." Jesus died a garbage-type death, yet he offered it to God. Anything and everything that consumes you and holds your focus is pulling you away from him. Ask Father to help you give it to him, memories, and pain, all of it. Each time a thought of it surfaces, remind yourself that you gave it to God and now it belongs to Him. Thank you Father for taking it, and using it the way he wants to.

A View of Sin

Focusing on sin is an idol--whether it's your sin or someone else's. It takes your focus off of God and puts it on the sin. In fact, when you are focusing on not sinning, you are not focusing on God. When you are focusing on loving God, you are focusing on loving God. That's how simple it is. Think how stressful it is to focus on controlling a sin. Now relax and focus on loving God.

1 Corinthians 6:9-10 gives a list of sins of people who will not enter heaven. Those 2 verses scare a lot of us, but continue to read on to verse 11 (MSG): "A number of you know from experience what I'm talking about, for not so long ago you were on that list. Since then, you've been cleaned up and given a fresh start by Jesus, our Master, our Messiah, and by our God present in us, the Spirit." That list of sins doesn't keep us out of heaven if we are believers, verse 11 says so. But sin injures our relationship with God. The good news shared in verse 11 says we believers have been cleaned up and given a fresh start. God sees us as clean. In his eyes, we are always going to have a fresh start.

Sin warps us so that we lean toward the negative things in life. God's love leans us toward him. Take a test and see if your view of sin is healthy or not. The next time you meet up with a person (any person will do), are your thoughts focused on what is right or what is wrong with them? Do you view him/her as God's loved child and see his beauty in him/her? Romans 5:21 (MSG) reveals the way God thinks about sin: "All sin can do is threaten us with death, and that's the end of it. Grace, because God is putting everything together again through the Messiah, invites us into life--a life that goes on and on and on, world without end."

Daddy Love

Some people have difficulty accepting God's goodness. I used to be one of those people. I didn't feel that I deserved God's goodness, so I didn't participate in any of the good accomplishments he had planned for my life. Yet, scriptures disprove that belief. I grew up listening to pastors who preached the only way to be humble was to remember how dirty and worthless we are because we are sinners. But the bible says that Jesus' blood has cleaned me up and has given me his worth. It's time to move on from the dirty/worthless life. I admit, it has been hard to shake off the old belief. My 21 Day Journal Notes helped to rewire my thinking to God's thoughts.

God's grace and goodness is evident in Romans 8:32 (GWT): "God didn't spare His own Son but handed him over [to death] for all of us. So he will also give us everything along with him." Jesus was the biggest good thing God could have given us, but this verse says he has more good things to give us.

Why wouldn't God want us to reach our full potential by using his goodness? God wants us to expect and receive his goodness. He has good plans for our lives and he is giving us every good thing we need to carry out his plans.

A while back, I was visiting Mom and Dad. I needed a pan to make popcorn in on the stove. I knew Momma had just the right old pan. I asked her if I could have it. I was thrilled with her reply. She said I could have anything I wanted, and I believed her! I recognize that same goodness in God. It's called Daddy-love.

Ephesians 1:5 (NIRV) reminds us of his Daddy's love: "So he decided long ago to adopt us as his children. He did it because of what Jesus Christ has done. It pleased God to do it." Did you feel the Daddy-love in that verse? It pleased him to give us Jesus! It pleases him to give us all the goodness we need to live out his plans.

Consider how living your life full of God's goodness allows others to see how good God is--in contrast to how bad Satan is as seen in the dumpster life.

In case you need more persuasion regarding accepting God's goodness, Romans 8:28 proves that God wants good for us. He wants good for us so much that he goes to the extreme to make our bad things into good things. Let that soak in. Here's the verse (NLT), if you're not familiar with it: "And we know that God causes everything to work together for the good of those who love God and are called according to his purpose for them." Notice he causes good for those who love him.

Because of his Daddy-love for you, he sees you as his well-loved child who loves him back. You are Daddy's girl/boy. Because of Jesus, you can accomplish anything that God has planned for you to do. He wants you to live the garden life. He is distressed when he sees you in an emotional turmoil. Turn to him and let him help you to health and well-being.

Every time I use momma's pan to make popcorn I think of her.

I remember her momma-love for me. I smile and enjoy the moment. God wants that from you, too. He has taught me that spending time with a person, talking and listening to another person, is what makes for a good relationship. That advise applies to him as well.

God showed me Daddy-love while I was writing this chapter. I procrastinated writing the first draft. I felt like the ideas would float into my mind then I would put them on paper. I watched an episode of Beth Moore's bible teaching (I was watching TV instead of writing). The first thing she said, as she looked into the camera, was, "You are at the end of the book and can't seem to finish it. You wonder why God isn't moving you. But God is wondering why you aren't finishing the book." I knew Daddy God was talking to me through Beth Moore. Funny thing is, it didn't feel like a scolding. I immediately sat down and started writing. He provided me with his thoughts as soon as I positioned myself to receive them.

Jesus is Husband Love

When Jesus came on the scene, he promoted a whole new way of life. It looks a lot like marriage. When two people get married the "me" becomes a "we." When we commit to Jesus, the "me" becomes a "we." Commitment and devotion is declared. The two partners move out of their parents' home and into a home of their own. New customs are learned from each other. The family and friend circle grows. Notice how the newness of life is birthed out of love, both in marrying partners and the Christian united with Jesus.

Towards the end of the wedding ceremony, the groom lifts the veil of his bride, exposing a woman with a new name, new life, and new purpose. Jesus lifted the veil for us, too. The very moment Jesus died on the cross the curtain separating the presence of man from the presence of God was torn in two. This happened inside the most holy place in the temple. That curtain was our bridal veil. Now, we are one with Christ.

The bible says that the church is the bride of Jesus. When you become a believer in Christ and decide to follow him, you are essentially vowing your love and commitment to him forever, through every phase of life. 2 Corinthians 11:2 (NIRV) introduces us as Mrs. Jesus Christ: "I promised to give you to only one husband. That husband is Christ. I wanted to be able to give you to him as if you were a pure virgin." This verse paints a mental picture of Daddy God giving his child away at the wedding ceremony. Did you notice the "pure virgin" part? That means he has made us clean and pure for Jesus.

Jesus died and rose again to new life so that we can be wedded to him and enjoy a fresh new married life. But the apostle Paul warns us of unfaithfulness on our part in verse 3 of 2 Corinthians 11: "But Eve was tricked by the snake's clever lies. And I'm afraid that in the same way your minds will somehow be led down the wrong path. They will be led away from your true and pure love for Christ." Notice how he is talking about our minds being led away from our love for Christ. So dear loved one, stay on the garden path. Keep your mind from wandering from your true love for Jesus.

The role of a husband is to take the wife's hand and walk in this new life together. The husband loves his wife. He encourages her to be healthy, happy and productive. The wife loves him back. She esteems him, respects him, and adores him. She is happy living with him. This is a beautiful picture of a marital relationship. Jesus speaks of this lovely relationship in John 14:23 (NIV): "Jesus replied, anyone who loves me will obey my teaching. My Father will love them and we will come to them and make our home with them." His teachings are the encouragements for you to be healthy, happy, and productive.

Consider your union with Jesus to be the greatest of all arranged marriages. God's goodness is what brought you together. Romans 2:4 (GWT) explains it this way: "Don't you realize that it is God's kindness that is trying to lead you to him and change the way you think and act?" You know me well enough by now to know that I'm going to point out the word "think" in this verse. Your garden life starts in the mind by changing the way you think over to his ways of thinking.

A New Love, A New You

Being married to Jesus has its benefits. You don't feel second rate anymore. He wants you to be the best you and he wants to help you achieve it. This marriage will never be hopeless as long as your mind is focusing on him and his teachings. He wants to keep you happy and content. You'll never feel like he's being unfaithful to you. He really wants you!

The first benefit is found in Matthew 10:39 (MSG): "If your first concern is to look after yourself, you'll never find yourself. But if you forget about yourself and look to me, you'll find both yourself and me." This verse is a bit of a mystery. It doesn't make sense that you can find your mate and yourself by focusing on your mate, yet with Jesus, that is what happens. In fact, by focusing on him you mysteriously become ok with yourself, even happy with who you are. I challenge you to find yourself today using his method!

The second benefit is explained in 1 Thessalonians 2:12 (MSG): "Holding your hand, whispering encouragement, showing you step-by-step how to live well before God, who called us into his own kingdom, into this delightful life." Don't you feel hope just by reading this verse? Imagine the reality of hope by holding his hand, listening to his whispered encouragements and using the step-by-step methods to live well before God. End result: delightful life, a garden life.

As far as his faithfulness is concerned, consider what Ephesians 1:11 (MSG) says: "It's in Christ that we find out who we are and what we are living for. Long before we first heard of Christ and got our hopes up, he had his eyes on us, had designs on us for glorious living." He's crazy over you and has been for a long time. He's never going to let you go. He has a garden life planned for you.

Authenticity sells and you can't sell Jesus to the public if you aren't in love with him. 1 Corinthians 16:14 (NLT) reports this: "And everything you do must be done with love." A full potential Christian makes Jesus look attractive. Would Jesus be attractive if you felt second-rate, hopeless and unwanted? Of course not--but these thoughts are from Satan, not Jesus.

At the end of the ceremony, the minister presents the newly wedded couple to the world in a grand announcement. Father does the same for us. James 1:8 (NLT) announces us this way: "He chose to give birth to us by giving us his true word. And we, out of all creation, became his prized possession."

Believe You Can Live the Garden Life

It is my experience that you can grow your faith in any area that

God has spoken of in the bible. I've given you several bible verses pointing to the fact that our Garden Life starts NOW! 2 Corinthians 5:7 (ERV) clarifies this truth about faith: "We live by what we believe will happen, not by what we can see." "Believe will happen" is another way of saying "having faith." Faith, belief, and trust are mental/spiritual muscles that can be exercised and strengthened--and grown larger than they previously were.

Proverbs 3:3 (NIRV) gives tips for how to grow these muscles: "Don't let love and truth ever leave you. Tie them around your neck. Write them on the tablet of your heart." Some translations use the term faithfulness in place of truth, but I think truth fits really well here because whatever we believe in is what we believe to be true. The love and truth written in this verse are God's love and truth. You learn to love and find the truth by writing God's word down. "Writing them on your heart" means you are implanting them in your mind. Yes, those 21 Day Journal Notes grow love and faith.

Proverbs 3:4 (ERV) gives details of how you'll experience the Garden Life: "Then God will be pleased and think well of you and so will everyone else." The growth of love and faith produces good relationships, reduces family friction, and brings you closer to God and closer to the real you.

Discharge Plan

You are ready to check out of the rehab center but the good doctor has some prescriptions for you. As he hands you these treatments he is asking you to fill them and compliantly take them.

1. Serious commitment with God. Desired results of this prescription are: A sense of purpose for your life. It allows your old life to die and new life to flourish.

2. Develop a relationship with God. Fill this by spending time conversing and listening to him. This is done by praying and reading the bible. Do this once a day for at least 15 minutes. Increase the length of time as needed. The results of this treatment are: Daily instructions for specific needs. Sunday becomes a free worship day (that's my favorite!).

3. Change your thinking over to God's thinking. This can be accomplished by bible verse memorization and handwriting God's word, once a day, times 21 days. You could call this a God-thought transfusion. Expect a mental miracle. You'll sin less

without having to think about sinning less. Fear and anger fade away and die off. You'll develop a softer tone of speaking to yourself. A pleasant surprise will rise up inside of you: God's outline for how your life should look and feel will come true for you!

4. Focus on loving God. This one will require a consultation with your counselor, Holy Spirit. Ask him to help you love God the way he wants you to. The effects of this session will help you to love others, and yourself. You'll be able to forgive the folks you haven't been able to forgive in the past.

5. Grow your faith in God in all the areas you read about in the bible. The next time you speak to your counselor, (Holy Spirit), you'll be giddy with confidence and the feeling of wellbeing.

6. Be thankful for everything, especially the bad things. You'll claim this prescription as a wonder drug when you feel empathy and compassion in place of the depression and bitterness.

Collectively, these prescriptions produce the Garden Life. Don't be surprised to notice how colors are more intense, and your sense of smell is heightened. Foods will taste richer and music will be "music" to your ears. Certain illnesses will resolve and you'll experience wholeness. But best of all, impossibilities will become possibilities.

The Garden Life is the reward you are given when you love Father, Jesus and Holy Spirit. It is the "Happily Ever After" life!

ABOUT WYNNDY WILSON

I was born a coastal girl in Eastern North Carolina and have settled in the mountains of North East Tennessee.

I am a lover of palm trees, the beach, words, yard sales, and butterflies. But my dearest loves are (other than Jesus Christ) my husband (Keevin), my daughter (Maria), my son (Cody), their spouses, and my bunch of grandchildren with more to come in the future.

I am a teacher of Biblical Mental Health, a women's event planner, have a knack for decorating, and I organize everything. I am currently the Women's Ministry Coordinator of the Holston Baptist Association.

I am a former nurse and I have worked in various aspects of the medical field. My nursing background has shaped my current endeavors. I include prescriptive-type advise in my writings and speeches.

I ask God to make all of my endeavors beautiful, whether it's an event, speech, or a book. And he makes all of them beautiful every time. Because I ask him to. Thank You Father!

Made in the USA
Lexington, KY
22 July 2019